Copyright © 2014 MLG Publishing
(A Division of Mascot Label Group)
First Published 2014 by MLG Publishing

Book designed by Paul Tippett and Adrian Andrews for Vitamin P
Author: Henry Yates and Walter Trout
Commissioning Editor: Ed van Zijl
Editor: Lisa Bardsley

ISBN: 978-90-822002-0-1

Mascot Label Group
PO Box 231
2630 AE Berkel
The Netherlands

Visit the website www.mascotlabelgroup.com

Photographs supplied by: Ross Halfin, Bert Lek, Kevin Nixon, Marie Trout, Paul Bergen, Jeff Katz, George Lyons, Jerzy Tauer, Lynnette Cooper Trout, Marco van Rooijen, Lisa Seifert, Heather Bryant, V.G. Jairam, Brittany Fay, Donna Trout, Lars Juul, Paul Levitton, Herman Nyhof, Austin Hargrave, Witold de Man.

Every effort has been made to trace the copyright holders of the photographs in this book but one or two were unreachable. We would be grateful if the photographers concerned would contact us.

Printed in the UK

RESCUED *from* REALITY

The life and times of Walter Trout

MLG

HENRY YATES AND WALTER TROUT

RESCUED *from* REALITY

The life and times of Walter Trout

HENRY YATES AND WALTER TROUT

I dedicate this book to my family who is the light of my life: Marie, Jonathan, Michael, and Dylan. And to those who formed me: Lynnette, Ed Trout, Sr., Ed Trout, Jr., and Ted Morris.

Walter and John at the North Sea Jazz Festival in 1986

Walter and John in Germany in 1999

FOREWORD

The first time I met and heard Walter was at a loose gathering of musicians who were about to go on the road as a re-incarnated Canned Heat. It was in a garage in the back of someone's house and the only reason I was there was to check out the idea of me joining them for a tour of the States and Canada.

By the end of the afternoon I was very much impressed by their new guitar player who not only had a very flamboyant approach to his instrument but exuded a larger than life personality. I won't say he was the deciding factor of me joining the band but he certainly seemed to guarantee that I would be in for a wild and crazy time.

In those days I was a strong believer in alcohol use and from the look of it Walter seemed to believe in all things above that and beyond! And so we hit the road. Over the next couple of months, I made up my mind that if he ever tired of working with Canned Heat that he would make a fine partner for Coco Montoya who was my regular guitarist. From the moment he came on board the two of them came to be a force to be reckoned with as they traded fiery solos back and forth.

One night when I had a bad throat and was about to cancel the gig, Walter and Coco suggested they could share vocal honors and fulfill the Bluesbreakers commitment. I croaked a feeble yes and I suppose from that moment on, Walter felt he could strike out on his own. He subsequently put a band of his own together and began making a name for himself in Europe with CD recordings to follow.

Many years have passed and since then he and I have embraced the joys of sobriety and continued on our separate paths in music. You now have in your hands a really solid book to enjoy and learn more about one of the most talented rock and blues players on the world's stage.

Keep on rockin' my friend!

John Mayall 2014

Walter and John (holding the Classic Album Award) at the Classic Rock Roll of Honour party

INTRODUCTION

My first encounter with Walter Trout was a phone interview for Guitarist magazine in June 2008. I'll never forget it. That day, Walter was one part philosopher, one part stand-up comedian, firing off wit, wisdom and solid-gold anecdotes with a charisma that left my ears ringing. I picked up the phone as a fan. I put it down as a disciple.

In the years since then, as our paths crossed for various magazine commissions, I would always chew over the same conundrum. In a world where cosseted TV personalities, lobotomised footballers and say-nothing pop marionettes stare blankly from the biography shelves, why has nobody written the book on Walter Trout…?

Well, six years down the line, here it is. With respect to my illustrious roll-call of past interviewees – Ozzy, Lemmy, Slash, Dave Grohl, Paul Weller, Jack White, Pete Doherty, Brian May – I don't believe anybody else has a backstory to beat Rescued From Reality. There are moments here as gaspingly funny as anything in rock 'n' roll folklore, from Walter's spat with Albert King over a backstage toilet, to his lost weekend wandering the streets of Costa Mesa, dressed in a gorilla suit and peaking on LSD.

But this book goes deeper than industrial-strength hellraising. There were also subjects that – I hope he won't mind me saying – brought Walter to tears and our sessions to a standstill, from his desperately dysfunctional childhood to the recent health issues that he's battling as I write these words. Through it all, I've been staggered by Walter's unflinching honesty and his desire to tell the real story, warts and all, whatever light it paints him in.

I'm honoured that Walter chose me as his collaborator, and privileged to have been given a front-row seat as these incredible tales poured out. I only hope my contribution does justice to the most fascinating man I've ever placed a dictaphone in front of.

I'd also like to thank my beautiful wife, Laura, and our two perfect children, Millie and Oliver, for supporting me during this incredible journey.

Enjoy the book.

Henry Yates, 2014

SAW MY MAMA CRYIN'

Welcome to paradise. The lights come up on an idyllic American beach town as imagined by a Hollywood set designer. The camera pans across an endless horizon, untainted azure skies and an ocean twinkling like a jewellery box. The soundtrack takes in the assorted laughs and hoots of holidaying families as they tramp the elegant seafront boardwalk and take in the entertainments. On a wireless radio somewhere, Perry Como's inescapable hit single If (They Made Me A King) plays for the hundredth time that day.

The scene is hardly life in the jungle. Nor is it the modern daze. This is Ocean City, New Jersey, and it is March 1951: the dawn of an era in American history that will be retrospectively described by politicians as the 'good old days'.

Admittedly, in the wider world, the golden age isn't quite living up to its billing. In politics, that same month, United States citizens Julius and Ethel Rosenberg are found guilty of Soviet espionage and sentenced to the electric chair. In the Korean War, United Nations

troops grind a bloody path to Seoul.

But for Walter Trout – born March 6th across the water in the faded East Coast resort of Atlantic City, to a small but receptive first-night crowd – early life in Ocean City is as blissful and unblemished as he will ever know it.

"Atlantic City was like a ghetto by the sea back then," recalls Walter, "but my family lived in Ocean City, this small island just to the south. It was this beautiful beach resort town. The Jersey shore is known for being wild and crazy,

but Ocean City was founded in the 1800s by Methodist missionaries, so you couldn't even go to a convenience store and buy a bottle of beer, or to a restaurant for a glass of wine. And that actually made it nice for families."

Ocean City changed with the seasons. Over long summers, tourists thronged the beaches, fed the local economy and admired the ornate music pier and the boardwalk whose construction in 1928 had been overseen by Walter's grandfather, John E. Trout (a gold plaque

marks his achievement to this day). "Summers there were incredible," he recalls. "When I was born, they brought me home from the hospital and put me in the arms of my brother, who said, 'He looks like a little elf – I'm going to call him Elfie'. The name stuck and until my early teens I was known by that name. As a young boy, I would run out of the ocean soaking wet, dive onto the beach, roll around, then walk around covered with sand. So on that beach, I became known as Elfie the Sand Rat."

Come winter, the crowds melted away to the mainland, leaving a hauntingly beautiful ghost-town and the negligible local population with the run of it. "Everything was closed," recalls Walter. "Just streets of boarded-up houses. You could go up onto that beautiful boardwalk on your bicycle and because of the wind, you could ride for miles without pedaling once. Now, getting back was difficult. After Christmas, everyone would take their trees to the beach, lay them in a giant pile, light them on fire and have a huge bonfire.

"We basically lived a block from the ocean, so this beautiful beach and boardwalk were our playground. There were tunnels under there, all sorts of little hiding places. Years later, at Collingswood High School, I had failed English, because they wouldn't let me write a report on The Grapes of Wrath by John Steinbeck, which they said was a dirty book. I was supposed to go to summer school in Collingswood, but I just said 'Fuck it', ran away, hitchhiked to Ocean City and slept under the boardwalk until my father found me."

This is Ocean City, and it is March 1951: the dawn of an era in American history that will be retrospectively described by politicians as the 'good old days'.

LIFE BOAT N⁰ 2

All my love
C.

Beyond the boardwalk, the ocean, where Walter's father took a literal approach to the phrase 'in at the deep end' for his infant son's first swimming lesson. "I remember, my dad and his buddy took me and another kid out in his fishing boat when I was three years old," he recalls. "They threw us into the bay, moved a hundred feet away and told us, 'Now swim to the boat'. By the time we got there, we'd learnt how to swim. We've sent our own kids to lessons and they go through all this bullshit: it took us about three minutes!"

As the episode implies, Edward Phillip Trout Sr was something of a character: an autodidact and renaissance man whose appetite for knowledge filtered into his son. "He loved learning," recalls Walter. "He read voraciously and knew everything about everything. You could discuss anything from plumbing to quantum physics with the guy. But he was pretty much a school drop-out.

"He'd finished high school, not gone to college. He spent some years in the military and he was basically a very skilled carpenter. He could build a house from scratch, and he did that for my mom when they got together.

"My mother, Lynnette, was incredibly educated. She'd graduated high school two years early as valedictorian of her class, and she became an English teacher because of her love of literature. After she taught English for a while, she realised what she really loved was books, more than being a policeman in class. So she became a school librarian. To the day she died, pretty much, she still went to college. Not to get degrees, but just out of a love of learning."

Academia was valued in the Trout household, but this was hardly a childhood spent with its nose in a book. For Edward and Lynnette, culture was not a theoretical concept for rote-learning, but a visceral force to be experienced from the front row. "My parents were pretty hip," says Walter, "and they did their utmost to expose me to everything.

"There was a lot of music and art. We went to tons of plays and musicals. My mother once took me to New York to see Richard Burton doing Hamlet on

Broadway. As a kid, they'd take me to all the black jazz clubs in Atlantic City. I saw everyone from Ray Charles and James Brown to Ahmad Jamal, and I remember being very influenced by my dad's big band records, by Miles Davis and John Coltrane."

As this cultural tsunami crashed over him, Walter briefly considered a career in the theatre. "But then they sent me to a summer camp at Somers Point," he recalls, "run by the parents of Peter Erskine, who grew up to be one of the great jazz drummers.

"While all the other kids were outside, all I wanted to do was sit in this big lodge, where they had a record player and a stack of 45s. They had Buddy

Holly, Jerry Lee Lewis, Chuck Berry, Little Richard. Even all the way back then, I wanted to hear rock 'n' roll instead of riding horses."

At this juncture, it's tempting to speculate where life might have blown Walter, both personally and professionally, had his early years held this happy course. Balanced individuals from stable backgrounds rarely make great artists. In some parallel universe, it's feasible that music might have become a casual downtime hobby, as opposed to a painkiller and lifeline.

The armchair psychologists must admit defeat. We'll never know. The cold, hard, tangible truth is that before he even reached the age of five, this utopian existence of sea and sun was interrupted by a line drawn in the sand, as both Walter and elder brother, Edward P. Trout Jr, became aware of storm clouds on the horizon at home. It's not too glib to suggest that as the good old days turned bad, and daily life began to crumble, Walter was simultaneously born as an artist and bluesman (albeit one not yet toting a Stratocaster).

Opposite: Walter: "When I was just a little guy, my father (Edward Phillip Trout Sr. also pictured) was a lifeguard on the beach in Ocean City. That's the boat they used to row out in and rescue people. It says 'No. 2' because that was the 2nd Street beach in Ocean City. They still have the same boats there."

Above: Walter: "That was taken on the Ocean City boardwalk at a photographer's studio. To me, I sure look a lot like my dad. It's not actually a colour photo: they used to take black-and-white pictures and sorta colour them in. I was a well-behaved young fella back then."

Divorce was not an uncommon dilemma faced by children in the 1950s, but that didn't make the fractious unraveling of Walter's beloved parents any less painful. "Their marital problems started at an early age," he remembers. "They just didn't make it. There's a lot of theories as to what went on with them. We don't know the full story, but it wasn't amicable. There was some violence and trauma, and at one point, it got so bad between them that they sent me away for some months to live with another family.

"Some years later, when I discovered the guitar, that literally kept me from ending up in an insane asylum. But when my parents started having problems, and heading towards divorce, the ocean became really important to me. As more turmoil happened at home, that beach and ocean became great friends and a sanctuary. I could go there and escape. Nobody there but me.

"I came upon this realisation that the ocean was as close as I could get to envisioning what God might be. If you went on a boat out to sea, all you saw was endless water. The light would shine onto it, and make these little diamonds, and I thought of those as people's souls coming into God. Years later, I wrote a song called Faithful, and the first verse is about how I felt."

Given the spiritual solace he took from the beach and ocean, it was a further wrench when the family unit splintered in 1958, with Edward Jr remaining in the custody of his father in Ocean City, while seven-year-old Walter relocated with Lynnette to South Jersey. Measured aesthetically, their new surroundings were not so bad. Mother and son came to rest in the picture-perfect farm town of Laurel Springs, surrounded by rolling cornfields and cool, clear lakes that children bombed into over summer. Under different circumstances, Walter might yet have clawed back what remained of his childhood innocence.

Fate had other plans. Juxtaposed against this sleepy bucolic backdrop came the shattering arrival of Walter's stepfather, and a period of uncertainty and anguish that marked the young man for life. To

retrospectively paint Ted Morris as a pantomime villain is to oversimplify his story. As Walter explains, this was a good man, broken by war and battling severe mental health issues: "My stepfather was a very interesting man. He was a poet, and incredibly literary. I remember sitting having Sunday breakfast in our kitchen, and he'd make a hat and sword out of newspaper and do the final scene from Hamlet, playing all the parts. He could recite entire volumes of Wordsworth and Robert Frost. So he and my mother had

really bonded over their love of literature, great writing and art.

"He had been raised a Quaker and he was a pacifist, but when World War II broke out, he considered it a just war – y'know, going to stop Hitler and the Japanese – so he renounced his pacifism and joined the marines. He survived, but he was a prisoner of war for a while and he had been tortured. The only story I ever heard him tell about his experience in the war, was about being buried in sand up to his chest by the Japanese, and they had stood around and pissed on his head."

In modern times, though soldiers still return traumatised from battle – and governments are criticised for failing to preempt the suicides that often follow – there is at least an acknowledgement of war's psychological fallout. "But they didn't know about post-traumatic stress disorder back then," says Walter. "You were just supposed to come home from war and be a man, go out and get a job, all of that. But my stepfather was haunted and tormented, and he was an alcoholic. He would drink, then freak out and get violent.

"My brother would come back and forth from Ocean City. I remember many times when my stepfather tried to kill us. One time, we were both holed up in my bedroom, and he was screaming 'Unlock the door!' We wouldn't, so he got an axe and chopped down the door – at which point, my brother held him off with a shotgun. Even now, years later, it's hard for me to describe the depth of terror and fear that my brother and I felt at these moments. Many times, he and I would jump off the second-floor balcony, split and go sleep in the woods. There were other times I would have to go stay with my dad for a while, just to get out of there. It was all my mom could do to get food on the table. So it was rough.

"Some years later, when we moved to Collingswood and I was a teenager, my stepfather, whose grip on reality was rapidly disintegrating, got the insane notion that I was having an intimate affair with my mother. We lived in a small apartment then, and it really got crazy. I would lock my bedroom door at night and move this large desk-sized stereo console up against the bedroom door. Without fail, at some period during the night, I'd hear Ted trying to get in, rattling the doorknob and pushing on the door. This began the insomnia that still plagues me to this day. I wrote a song about it called Collingswood and recorded it on the Relentless album. It's a perfect example of how music has provided me a release and a therapeutic outlet.

"When it started getting really violent and his problems really started coming to the surface, my mother would leave him. She left him a few times, but he would turn up and beg her forgiveness. She'd take him back, he'd be OK for a couple of months, and then – boom – he'd go off again. So he was this very sensitive fellow who had been fucked over. And the amazing thing is, to this day, I still love the guy and I understood his mental problems."

Above: Walter: "I was sitting down playing in a field of long grass. My neighbour was swatting around with a baseball bat: he didn't see me and he pretty much knocked me out. That photo was taken a long time after. Just one of many wonderful childhood experiences…"

Even in these dark times, music broke through like a sunbeam. Passive enjoyment had evolved into participation, and Walter remembers his first aptitude was for jazz trumpet: "I took lessons from age six and I was pretty good at it. I could solo, and the licks I play on guitar now, I was hearing in my head and figuring out on the trumpet back then. I could read music and play the charts. That meant I got out of a lot of physical-ed bullshit at school. It was like, 'You can either play trumpet in the school band, or you can go run around the track for an hour'."

The clincher was an encounter with the Duke Ellington Orchestra on Walter's tenth birthday in 1961. "We drove down to the box office, and all these cars start pulling up with well-dressed black men getting out holding horn cases," he recalls.

"We realise that it's Duke Ellington and his orchestra, and there's Tony Bennett, and they're going inside. So we walked around to the back of the venue and my mom – she was fearless – knocked on the stage door. She said, 'My son is an aspiring trumpet player and it's his birthday. Is there any way Mr Ellington would give him an autograph or say hello…?'

"So we were escorted into this huge dressing room. I met all the guys, and it blew their minds, because I knew all their shit, while other ten-year-old white kids back then were listening to Frankie Avalon and Bobby Rydell. Then I was escorted over to this white couch, and there was Duke Ellington. I sat down, and we proceeded to have this incredible talk, where he told me about the music business, and how not to get caught up

in the hype or fame, or the stardom and glitz, because that was very fickle. He said to me, 'If you go into this, there'll be hangers-on who'll latch onto your coattails, and you just need to keep your focus on being an artist, because that's a noble pursuit'.

"I didn't realise that much charisma could exude out of people. It seemed to me that these guys knew a secret nobody else did. Right away, I wanted to know that secret too. How could you become *that* fucking cool…?"

This page: There's no cattle rustling in Ocean City with Sheriff Trout in charge. Walter: "That's as close as I've ever got to exercising my second-amendment rights here in the United States. I think that was probably taken around 1956, when I was five. My dad built that house and the fence, and it's still there. The people who own the house have kept it in good shape."

COLLINGSWOOD

My mama didn't worry
What the neighbors were thinking
Didn't have time for that stuff
We were livin' with a man
Who spent all day drinkin'
He was big, he was mean and rough

She was doin' her best just to raise her boy,
up to be a man
But when I looked at the violence in our home
I told mama that I didn't understand

She said, It's all right, it's all right, it's all right
Someday it's gonna be all right

Each day I wondered
Will we make it till tomorrow?
With all what's goin' on
The axes and the shotguns
The whiskey and the sorrow
Will we make it to the dawn

I'd lie there in my bed
All night shakin'
I was fearin' for my skin

I'd move the furniture
Against the bedroom door
To keep the big man from gettin' in
And my brother told me

It's all right, It's all right, It's all right
Someday it's gonna be all right

Well, it was so long ago
But it still affects me
And sometimes I wake up in a sweat
And I lay there remembering that small boy
As scared and lost as I could get
Out of the darkness comes a vision
And I wonder what it is I see
Then I realize it's the spirit of my mama
And she puts her arms around me
And she says

She says It's all right, It's all right, It's all right
Someday it's gonna be all right

TRANSITION

So there was the question. How, indeed, could you become *that* fucking cool? As he staggered starry-eyed from Duke Ellington's couch, the answer popped in the air above Walter's head like a cartoon lightbulb. Become a professional musician, of course. Cut a stream of era-defining records. Travel the world in search of swashbuckling adventure. For a troubled ten-year-old with neither band nor contacts, however, the path to that utopia had no signposts.

The afterglow of meeting Ellington ensured that, for a time, Walter stuck with brass. "When I was twelve, my mother said to me, 'There's this drum and bugle corps that practises right down the street: why don't you go down there with your trumpet?' It turned out to be this New Jersey State Champion corps named The Vagabonds. I was accepted in as a bugler, and found myself marching in major stadium parades. I was suddenly in a society of kids where you were valued for your artistic contribution, not for throwing a fucking football. Plus, I got to travel in a bus all summer and see what that whole road-gypsy life was like. It was an important part of my coming-up."

Yet his allegiances were shifting. In the decade between Walter's birth and his adolescence in the 1960s, music and its associated culture had taken giant leaps, from the big bands and buttoned-up crooners of the post-war era, via rock 'n' roll trailblazers like Chuck Berry, to game-changing wordsmiths like Bob Dylan. Noting the common denominator of the new breed – guitar – a fateful move was to trade his weapon of choice. "As far as playing guitar," he recalls, "that

really came about during the folk music movement. The Chad Mitchell Trio and Peter, Paul and Mary. Then my brother brought back Bob Dylan's first album in '62 and told me, 'You gotta hear this guy'. That was it."

Just as pivotal was Edward Trout Jr's arrival with the cheap acoustic guitar on which Walter would plant his first

artless chord shapes. Then, like annual thunderbolts, came The Beatles in 1964, Paul Butterfield's eponymous 1965 debut and the 1966 album from John Mayall's Bluesbreakers, dubbed 'Beano' for its cover shot of Eric Clapton thumbing the comic of the same name, and feted for the young guitarist's amp-burning riffs within.

Electricity, realised Walter as he devoured his brother's trophies, was the future: "That Butterfield album changed my life. The first time I heard it, I remember heavily and vividly. The room and the stereo we played it on…"

At that point, the beat-to-hell Fender Stratocaster that would one day be immortalised on his solo album sleeves was still blissfully sprouting from the earth. Like most fledgling guitarists, then and now, Walter got onto the bottom rung of the property ladder: "My first electric guitar was some cheap little thing like a Kent, and I had a Silvertone, which is a company made by Sears and Roebuck. These guitars were made out of plywood, and I had one where your amp was this little speaker in the case.

"But the first guitar I really wanted was a Fender Telecaster, because Mike Bloomfield had played one on the first Paul Butterfield album. Now, Teles were, like, $150. So I started saving my money. But then, when I had enough money to get the Tele, out came Super Session with Mike Bloomfield in '68, and he had a Gibson Les Paul, which meant I had to get one. Les Pauls were $220. I didn't know shit about guitars, but I knew I needed more money, so my grandmother went over to 8th Street Music in Philadelphia with me and she covered the difference."

Guitar became the focus, as the rest of Walter's world receded. It was, he remembers, the final nail in a once-promising school career that had been bombed into freefall by his parents' divorce and the passive-aggressive mania of life with his stepfather. "When we graduated the eighth grade in '65, I was voted most likely to succeed. I had dreams of being a lawyer or going into politics, changing the world and becoming an activist.

"I was even the guy that delivered the graduation speech for the class. I wrote this big speech about the future of the country and the government, about how Lyndon Johnson was bringing in creeping socialism and how we had to go to Vietnam and fight to stop communism. I was a raging right-wing Goldwaterite. I was flying the flag, man, USA all the way.

"But little by little, I turned from Barry Goldwater into a raging hippie. It started with the Kennedy assassination, and then figuring out that what the government was telling us was bullshit. Then I went to Collingswood High School in 1965 and met a fellow named Richard Ormsbee, who had long talks with me and convinced me the war was wrong. The more life got crazy with my stepfather, the more I got disillusioned with the world and school. I didn't want to listen to authority anymore. Like many of my generation in the 1960s, I

just went into that thing of, y'know, I'm just gonna sit around and play the guitar, and fuck it.

"At that point, I couldn't take this Elfie bullshit anymore and I started trying to get everybody to call me Walter. So around the age of 14, the whole Elfie thing went away, even though the Trouts back in New Jersey still call me by that name. Later, when I did a Jenny Craig commercial in 1994, they saw me on TV and they were like, 'Oh my God – that's Elfie!' They got in touch with Jenny Craig and we had a little reunion."

Ormsbee was just one of a new cast of compadres. "When I lived in Laurel Springs, I didn't know anybody that cared about music," remembers Walter. "They all wanted to play football, be macho and shit. Then I met Jack Jeckot at Collingswood. It was like meeting Paul McCartney. The guy was a virtuoso on every instrument. He showed me my first guitar leads. It almost used to piss me off. But he was the coolest guy I ever met, because he didn't care about peer pressure. It rolled over him like water off a duck that he wasn't an athlete, in this school that was so devoted to athletics. He was so secure in his skin, whereas after the divorce, I was very lost and just kinda floundering through life. So I hooked up with him, and as far as I was concerned, he and I were gonna be Lennon and McCartney.

"There was also Delphene Langran. I met her in ninth grade. She was my age, but she was the accompanist of the school choir I was in. We hit it off immediately, and me and Jack started hanging out at her house. She had an old 1920s National Steel Duolian, which is the blues guitar of Son House and Bukka White. It had been in her family for years, and I would sit in her living room and play it, and she'd even let me take it home. We're still great friends, and she loaned me the guitar for the cover photo of The Blues Came Callin'.

Opposite: Lynnette Trout, 1965
Above: The first photo of Walter and an electric guitar in 1966

"Delphene was my first passionate love. I've only had two in my life. She changed my life. She showed me that I could be loved for who I am. She was classy, she loved art, literature and going to museums, and she played piano wonderfully. She was the one that inspired songs like Earrings On The Table, The Mountain Song and The Love That We Once Knew. She moved to California, eventually, to get away from me, and the last thing she said to me on the phone was, 'Walter, I'll always love you, but I don't need you in my life any longer'. And I took that phrase and wrote the song Frederica."

Walter's new crew might have soothed his internal torment, but they couldn't cure it. From disillusionment, he recalls, it was a short hop to drugs. "I was a bit of a lost individual, trying to find my way through life, somewhat mentally damaged and afraid. I'd already got drunk a few times aged 15, and I didn't particularly like it, but the first actual drug I ever did was LSD. This Ormsbee had run away and hitchhiked to California, hung out with The Grateful Dead and met Owsley Stanley, the guru of LSD. He'd come back with some white Owsleys. A lot of guys start off by smoking pot: I started with the strongest acid on the face of the earth. So that was a rude awakening.

"We all went out into the park at 1am, and lay down under the gazebo. I experienced that I was on the beach in Ocean City. It was daylight and there were blue skies and people all around. Then, in my brain, the police came and busted me, because I was on acid, and

took me to jail. I went to court, stood up in front of the judge, got bailed out by my parents. None of this actually happened, but I experienced it completely. So that was my first experience with drugs. After that, I

started smoking cannabis every day for years."

Music, too, was a growing habit. "When I was about eighteen," remembers Walter, "I heard about a coffee house called the Perimeter on the campus at Rutgers University, Camden.

It was a tiny place devoted to folk music, operating every Friday night, and I started driving up there with my friends, and even managed to get up and play. I did Earrings On The Table and a few others, and I became a staple there as the on-call guitar player. As a matter of fact, I made my first-ever recording there, doing Earrings On The Table on the live album, A Night At The Perimeter, which is still around.

"The Perimeter was very pivotal in my life. It was started by Pete Curry. Later, Jim Herd took over the management and gave me a key because I kept running away from home and having nowhere to sleep. It was on campus, in the basement of classroom buildings; nobody lived around there.

"So I could go down there at midnight, take my amplifier, set it up on the stage and lock the door. Then I'd take a hit of LSD and I could play for twelve hours at a stretch, at rip-roaring volume, without bugging anybody. I would do that until I passed out on the stage, wrapped around my Fender amplifier."

But at the tail-end of the 1960s, Walter's soft-focus existence of music and hallucinogens was interrupted by real life banging hard at the door. In distant lands, Vietnam still raged, and the US war machine's turnover of fresh meat was insatiable. It's estimated that 3.5 million servicemen were deployed to South-East Asia between 1964 and 1975, and many came via the draft: a system of conscription dating back to colonial times that demanded enrolment of all able-bodied men in times of national emergency.

With upward of 58,000 Americans killed in action over that same period, there was every chance the return journey would be made in a wooden box. "When I was in The Vagabonds, I had met a musician named Bill Hamacher," recalls Walter. "The day he turned 18, he enlisted, went to Vietnam, and shortly after, his entire platoon was wiped out in an ambush. It took me thirty years to write the song Bugle Billy about him, and the story is true in that lyric. I only sang it once in the studio, then I broke down."

Faced with those statistics, it's understandable that in the late-1960s, entrepreneurial young shirkers of every stripe were dreaming up ingenious ways to avoid Vietnam. Walter's own tactic was relatively prosaic: "Well, I just didn't turn up to register. I thought, 'Fuck it, they don't need to know I exist'. Later, when I was 21, my father, who'd been a military policeman, said 'Hey Walt, what are you doing about the draft?' When I admitted I hadn't registered, he went through the roof and told me I had two weeks or he was gonna call up and report me.

"So I went in, and they told me that because I was three years late, this was a felony. They said that in two weeks, I had to go before the draft board – which is these ten rich old men in suits who send poor kids away to get their asses blown off – and I could go to federal prison.

"So for those two weeks, I didn't bathe. Didn't brush my teeth. Didn't comb my hair. Didn't change my clothes. Took LSD every day. The morning of my meeting at the draft board, I took some more LSD, and I stumbled in there, stinking, funky and

greasy. They talked to me for about ten minutes, before they put me in a classification where they would draft a quadriplegic or an 85-year-old lady before me. If you were classified as '1A', that means you're outta here. I was '1H',

which stands for 'holding', and that means you're bottom of the barrel. When everyone else in the country has been killed, *then* they'll call you. So I was now signed up for the draft, but they didn't want to know about me. Which really embarrassed my dad."

With the military off his back and jungle warfare averted, Walter was free to pursue his first professional band and quantifiable step into the music industry. Pull up a stool and order a beer in any Jersey taproom of the early-1970s and you wouldn't have waited long for the arrival of Wilmont Mews: the band whose seeds had been sown back at Collingswood. "All through high school, Jack Jeckot was working, playing gigs, starting these different bands," explains Walter. "I remember one of them was called Cold Beer. When he got out of high school, he went to a music school outside Philly and that's where he met all these guys who played the horns in what became Wilmont Mews.

"That band was also where I met Dan Araco, who was a friend of the bass player. His uncle was Albert Anastasia, who ran the mob in New York City and was famously gunned down in a barber's chair. Dan became like a brother to me over the years, and as far as the main male friend I've had in my life, he's the one.

"He started working for Wilmont Mews as the sound guy, and we ended up living together, with some other musicians, in a house in South Jersey we called Commando Headquarters. The reason being, we didn't have money for food, so we'd go out at night to all-night supermarkets and steal steaks by putting them down our pants. We called those commando raids, we were known as the commandos, and our house was known as HQ.

Opposite: Walter's first love, Delphene Langran
Above: A young Walter suited and booted

"Wilmont Mews was a really great band. We did covers of Stax and Motown. We'd even do stuff like take Brown Sugar by the Stones and turn it into a horn line song, or take Satisfaction, but do the Otis Redding version where the horns play the Keith Richards guitar part.

"One of my funniest memories is that for our first gig, we played a big Christmas party for deaf-mutes. There were four hundred of them in this room, and the guy that hired us said, 'Play as loud as you can, because they can feel the vibrations of the music'. It was great, man. We had everything cranked up to ten and they were having the time of their lives.

"Halfway through the night, they had a dinner, and there were four hundred people in a room eating and nobody was talking. It was dead silent, so every once in a while, one of us in the band would just yell out, 'Fuck!' and everyone would just keep on eating. It really was an amazing experience. But I always thought it was somewhat of an omen for that band, that our very first show, we played to a roomful of people that couldn't hear us."

Wilmont Mews could have been contenders: that much is clear from the band's neck-tingling take on So Sad To Be Lonely, performed in a Jersey bar circa 1972 and featured retrospectively on 2005's Deep Trout compilation. From that surviving track, it's obvious, too, that Walter's soul-in-fingers lead work was already in a league above the sloggers. "On that early-'70s circuit, I was like the hot-guitar-player guy," he says. "Everybody knew that Wilmont Mews had this lead player, and it was one of the band's selling points."

Walter's prowess also meant he recognised when rivals weren't up to snuff. "We played all up and down the Jersey shoreline," he recalls, "where there was this whole circuit of nightclubs and constant music. We did many nights with a band called Steel Mill, and that was Bruce Springsteen with what later became the E Street Band. I thought they were good. I didn't think they were any better than us. Bruce could always sing really good, but he was supposed to be the lead guitar player and he couldn't play very well. We'd be hanging out, drinking and shit in the parking lot, and I used to tell him, 'Man, your guitar solos suck. You've gotta work on your playing, y'know, because as soon as you go off into a solo, it fucking hurts your ears, man. You're not bending the strings, you're not hitting the notes, go work on your vibrato…'.

"So I'd give him all this, and I remember Bruce saying one time, 'Well, I'm starting to write songs…'. I was shit-faced and told him, 'Man, I hope you write some good ones, 'cos you ain't gonna make it as a lead guitar player!'"

The outward bravado belied Walter's doubts over his own career. Like countless bar bands, before and since, Wilmont Mews were a solid live draw when they stuck to brass-fuelled covers of radio hits, but saw crowds dwindle when they floated original material. "As long as we were playing covers with the big horn line we were incredibly popular," explains Walter. "But I took over the band, turned it into a four-piece, started writing original songs and fronting it. As soon as that happened, we couldn't get a fucking gig."

Walter couldn't shake the growing sense that New Jersey was a small pond where the fantastical odds of breakthrough were longer still. There had already been signs of itchy feet. In the summer of 1970, he had taken a trip to Chicago, smelt possibilities on the Windy City's vibrant club scene and almost taken the plunge. "That's one of the big what-ifs in my life," he remembers. "But the historical context was that we were still not even two years past the assassination of Martin Luther King. When he was killed in 1968, all the major US cities rioted and burned. So it was a scary time for race relations, and the thought of me, aged 19, going to live in the south side of Chicago, wondering if I'd survive just walking down the street… that made me chicken out."

As Walter explains, it took one of the most traumatic incidents of his early life

to give the decisive push. "Wilmont Mews couldn't get a gig, so I had to get day jobs, and I actually spent time as a drug counselor in Philly. I'd been hired by this programme that was trying to rehabilitate junkies, not only through group therapy, but through the arts. It was an experiment by the National Institute of Mental Health at the Thomas Jefferson University.

I was hired to run the music programme. I basically had a junkie band. I had this huge room full of instruments. I'd show one guy how to play Louie Louie on the bass. I'd teach another guy the drumbeat. Then we'd play Louie Louie for

Wilmont Mews could have been contenders: that much is clear from the band's neck-tingling take on So Sad To Be Lonely, performed in a Jersey bar circa 1972 and featured retrospectively on 2005's Deep Trout compilation. From that surviving track, it's obvious, too, that Walter's soul-in-fingers lead work was already in a league above the sloggers.

forty-five minutes, and they'd get the therapeutic feeling of putting an amp way up and pounding on a guitar."

Yet the role came with heavy responsibility: "People would come to the programme out of prison. If you'd been in the programme for a year and stayed clean, you could get out of your sentence and you were free. But if you got dirty urine tests, you had to go back to prison. So I was basically having to send people to prison when they didn't do good. There was one kid. He was about sixteen. He had a girlfriend, he'd got her pregnant,

and they were living in an abandoned house in Philadelphia. So he started doing the only thing he could to make money: dealing drugs in the programme, which was the ultimate, cardinal sin. I had to take this kid into a room and tell him I was sending him back to prison, at which point he basically attacked me and tried to kill me. He went home that night and hung himself.

"After that, I basically had a nervous breakdown. It was just too hard for me to go home at five each night, having watched all the human suffering going on amongst these people, and just turn it off. All those professionals supposedly knew how to do that, but I didn't know how. All I wanted to do was play the guitar, for fuck's sake.

"So the kid hung himself. And that's when I said, 'Fuck this'. I'd been out to California on a vacation and seen bands like mine that were working. I'd gone back to Jersey and said to the guys that we ought to go out there. We kept on discussing it, and one-by-one they all chickened out. But when that kid hung himself, it was the catalyst. At that point, I just thought, 'Enough is enough. If you guys don't want to go out there, I'll go on my own and see what I can do'. There was nothing left for me in Jersey or Philly anymore.

"Before I left for California, I drove to Ocean City to see my dad and say goodbye. The next morning, I went down to the beach where I had spent my beautiful, idyllic young years. I sat in the sand, I watched the diamonds on the water, I thought about my life, and reaffirmed to myself who I was and what I was here for. I knew I needed to get in my VW Bug and drive west, following the sun, leaving behind all I knew and entering a new world yet unknown. As I stood up, wiping the sand off my clothes, I looked at the sea and I said, 'It's time for Elfie the Sand Rat to become Walter the guitar player.'"

Opposite: A 20-year-old Walter and Wilmont Mews in 1971

LOOKIN' FOR THE PROMISED LAND

There follows an inventory of Walter Trout's possessions, stowed in his Volkswagen Beetle upon departure for the West Coast in 1974. One Gibson ES-335 semi-electric guitar. One Martin D-28 dreadnought. One Fender Super Reverb amplifier. One trumpet. One mandolin. Thirty tabs of LSD, a half-pound of marijuana concealed within the door-frame, and $150 wadded in his back pocket. Less tangible, though fuelling his progress on the coast-to-coast trek, was the derision of his ex-bandmates. "They all sat around and laughed, waiting for me to come back," he remembers. "I just told them, 'I'll see ya'. I drove eleven days across the country by myself, camping in a little tent."

Walter's narcotic-laden Bug puttered into Costa Mesa, California, on October 31st – Halloween – where the guitarist was greeted by his hosts with news of a costume party that evening, and the offer of a full-body gorilla suit if he cared to join them. "So I put on the suit, with nothing on underneath it other than my underwear. Then I gave everybody a tab of LSD and off we went. I was in this Halloween party when the LSD started taking effect, and I started having what you would call a clichéd bum trip. I started freaking out and thinking I had made a huge mistake driving to California. I left the party and started walking, but I'd never been to this town before, and pretty soon I realised I didn't know how to get back to the house. So there I was, peaking on LSD, walking around Costa Mesa, lost and wearing a gorilla suit.

"I walked into this little café, sat down at the counter, took my gorilla head off and set it next to me. The waitress came over to ask if she could get me something and I just started crying uncontrollably. I told her, 'I don't have any money. I'm lost. I'm on acid. And I'm ready to jump off a building'. Well, she got me a cup of coffee, calmed me down and asked if I knew the name of the street the house was on. I told her, and she gave me easy directions. She saved my life that night. I made it back to the house, still in the gorilla suit.

"A few years later, I was playing in California and there's this girl in the audience. She's looking at me and I'm looking at her, and in the end, I go 'I know you from somewhere'. She goes, 'My God… you're the gorilla!' And she was the waitress who'd saved my life that night. Anyway, that was my first night in California. Lost, on really strong LSD, wearing a gorilla suit."

WEST

INTERSTATE
CALIFORNIA
8

Enough monkey business: Walter needed a gig. Ostensibly, this should have been easy. California circa 1974 was the hub and heart of the US music industry. At its highest echelons, this was a sunkissed utopia where A-list stars descended from their mansions in the Hollywood Hills to bottle billion-sellers at iconic studios like the Capitol Building and Record Plant. For now, all that was a world away from the guitarist's reality. Beneath rock's big fish milled the bottom-feeders: a substratum of wetbacks and sloggers who plied their anonymous trades in sticky-floored bars across the sunshine state.

"I got into this country band who had a house gig at a restaurant in Corona Del Mar," remembers Walter. "They were great players, but not one of them could sing. I went up to them and said, 'Hey, I know every fucking song that Hank Williams, Merle Haggard and Buck Owens ever wrote'. So I'm standing up there at the mic singing Merle Haggard tunes, and with my third paycheck, I bought the Strat that's still on the cover of all my CDs. It is quite literally the heaviest guitar I've ever lifted. It's heavier than a Les Paul. I don't know how I wore it for so many years."

It wouldn't be accurate to suggest live music was Walter's sole revenue stream in those early years on the West Coast. Servicing two needs at once – sex and money – 1975 saw him cohabiting with a statuesque blonde girlfriend, who also happened to have a thriving drug-dealing business in Redondo Beach. Walter's gift of the gab made him the ideal concierge for clients picking up their fixes: "I was her 'business partner'. She'd go out and leave me all these pre-measured packets of hard narcotics for her customers. They were all packaged and sat on the shelf by the front door, like candy bars or something. Somebody would knock and I'd open up: 'Hey Frank, how you doing?' He'd go, 'I want $100-worth of this' and I'd hand it out the door."

While his guitar skills had yet to ignite the West Coast, Walter soon discovered that a sack of narcotics was a skeleton

key that could unlock any showbiz door in California. "My girlfriend took me a party in LA one night," he remembers, "and there was Jesse Ed Davis.

"I was a big fan of his. I had spent hours listening to the first couple of Taj Mahal albums, and he'd done all the guitars, piano and even horn arrangements on there. My girl came over to me and said, 'I was just talking to Jesse and he's looking for either a rhythm guitarist or a keyboard player'."

Davis was patently in a different stratosphere to this arm-chancing

interloper from New Jersey, but that didn't stop Walter turning on industrial-strength charm. "I went over and said, 'Hey Jesse, my name's Walter and I'd like to try out for your band'. He asked who I'd played with, and I had to tell him I'd just played with a bar band in Jersey, to which he said, 'Well, I played with John Lennon, Rod Stewart and Bob Dylan'. So I said to him, 'Look, let me come to a practice, just play two songs… and I'll bring a big bag of dope'."

Open sesame. "So I went to a little rehearsal hall in Venice, California, in 1975. I brought along the dope, and I played, and I remember that Jesse went, 'Well, fuck, you can play *and* you've got all

these drugs. You're in the band'. So all of a sudden, this was a happening LA band. I was playing up and down the Sunset Strip, doing the Starwood club and all these cool gigs up there in Hollywood. I'd been thrust into the fast lane."

Heroin might have opened the door, but it also dashed any chance that this late-period Davis outfit would leave a lasting thumbprint on the rock 'n' roll annals. By this point in the mid-1970s, the drug already had the bandleader in a tailspin – he would ultimately meet his tawdry end in 1988, OD'd on the floor of a Venice laundry room – while Walter had broken the golden rule of the successful dealer and was getting high on his own supply.

"Heroin was hard to get off," he admits. "I knew I had to quit, so I started going to a methadone clinic. They gave you a little glass of orange juice with a dose in there, and gradually decrease your dosage every day. I used to drive Jesse up there; he'd do his methadone and then buy heroin from my girlfriend, so he had two habits going.

"I'd drive all these different musicians, like Gregg Allman, or Joe Lala, who played congas in Stephen Stills' band. One day, I went into the clinic and drank my juice, and the guy said, 'You just drank pure orange juice – you're clean'."

It was time to cleanse the rest of his life. In 1977, around the same time as kicking heroin, Walter also drew a line under dealing it, perhaps as much through an attack of nerves as conscience. Business was good, but things had got heavy. As Walter explains, FBI heat was on two of his girlfriend's associates, Christopher Boyce and Andrew Daulton Lee – soon to be jailed for selling US state secrets to the Soviet Union – and the danger of being caught in the closing net was palpable. "One day, near the end of my methadone course, there was a knock at the door and it was two guys in suits: 'Hi Walter, we're the FBI'. I had my jaw on the ground, because there was $10,000-worth of hard narcotics within three feet of them – and because they knew my name.

"So these guys tell me, 'We want you to know that we've just arrested your friends, Daulton Lee and Christopher Boyce, for espionage. We've been watching them for a year, and due to watching them, we know everything you're doing. We just thought you'd like to know that'. Then they walked away. It wasn't more than a couple of days later that I got the fuck out of there. That happened to coincide with the end of the methadone clinic. So I told my girlfriend I'd got a gig in Huntington Beach, took my guitar and amp, and never went back. The FBI could have pursued that, but they didn't. Some years later, Daulton Lee and Christopher Boyce were immortalized in the book and movie titled The Falcon and the Snowman."

There was still an apology owed to Walter's beloved mother, who had suffered her son's slide from sandy-haired cherub into glass-eyed, rail-thin junkie without ever cutting him adrift. "There had been no way to hide my addiction from her," he says, "and after I had kicked heroin, I went up and saw her. We took a long walk in the woods in Coos Bay, Oregon, where my mom had retired with my stepfather in tow, and I told her about my heroin addiction, and how I was fucked-up.

"She didn't judge me, she didn't scold me. She just held my hand as we walked, and it was a beautiful moment. I was still fucked-up for years after that. But I'd kicked heroin, and I came back to Huntington Beach to try and be a guitar player, instead of a drug dealer."

Perhaps, somewhere in his subconscious, Duke Ellington's warning to avoid the hype and glitz still echoed. When Walter resurfaced from the Davis debacle – following a period of borderline vagrancy that saw him crashed on the couches and garage floors of patient friends – it was 1977, and his latest band was the decidedly grass-roots Midnight Angel. "We had a residency at this little club in Costa Mesa called The Mustang Ranch," he says. "It was an incredible band, but the problem was that we tried to be a democracy. We had five lead singers, a whole bunch of songwriters, and onstage we'd argue over who was gonna sing the next song. That's when I realised that if I ever did go solo, I was gonna be the dictator and the guys in my band could either groove with that or get another gig. There has to be a fearless leader."

Opposite: The heroin days
This page: Mixing it up with Midnight Angel at The Mustang Ranch, 1977

In retrospect, Midnight Angel's greatest significance was that its lineup featured one Jimmy Trapp: the human hurricane who would become Walter's solo-era bassist and wingman, and whose genius on the instrument was matched only by his flair for mayhem. The pair bonded immediately. "The first road trip we ever took as Midnight Angel, Jimmy and I had great ambitions," remembers Walter. "We'd been invited to Sun Valley, Idaho, where this promoter supposedly had us booked in for two weeks in a nightclub, topped off with this big outdoor concert in an amphitheatre. We were going to open for the Amazing Rhythm Aces, who had a bunch of hits in America back then, and the show was going to be called Aces In The Bowl.

"So we take a ride up there with some friends. But when we get there, the promoter tells us, 'The club gig has fallen through, but if you stick around for two weeks, you can still do the gig in the amphitheatre'. So now, we didn't have a way to get home, which we hadn't quite figured out when we went up there. We're stuck. We don't have any work or money. Our keyboard player, Danny Timms – who went on to play twelve years with Bonnie Raitt – spent a couple of nights sleeping on a bench on Main Street, Ketchum. Me and Jimmy ran into this guy who owned a dog kennel, and he said, 'Look, if you guys come and play for my buddies at the barbecue in my back yard on Sunday afternoon, you can each have your own cage.'"

Raw though it was, the deal was done: "So we played for him and we got our own little cage in this kennel. These cages were about three feet high, and there were dogs all around us on either side,

barking all night. So me and Jimmy would go into our little cages and sleep on the ground. We had to ask the guy if he had a pillow or a blanket. To eat, we'd borrow the guy's fishing rod and walk half a mile to a river, then he would let us cook the fish."

Given the grim circumstances, perhaps some reality-altering drugs were forgivable. "One night," remembers Walter, "Jimmy and I just couldn't stand the cages, the barking and the dog-shit any longer, and somehow we procured some LSD and a bottle of Jack Daniel's. We ate the LSD and went out on the main drag of Ketchum, the yellow line between us, hallucinating and passing the bottle back and forth, telling ourselves how this is not gonna get us down, and we are gonna do something with music. That, granted, this trip is fucked, but we have some talent and we're gonna fucking stick with this. That's a big memory for me of Jimmy: the pair of us tripping on acid and swearing a solemn oath to be lifelong troubadours."

Days later, a lifeline: "So Aces In The Bowl does finally happen. We're gonna play this outdoor gig at this amphitheatre, so we're all worked-up and inspired, man, because it's a big gig with a national band and all this. But we go out there, we start playing – and we've only played three songs before the promoter

comes out and says, 'Look, we're gonna have a wedding onstage, so you guys need to cut your set short…'"

Teeth were duly gritted as the band filed into the promoter's office for their fee. "We needed that money to get home," says Walter, "but now the guy tells us, 'Oh, I don't have any money for you, but I do have this big pile of cocaine, so why don't you guys just snort some?' I remember, at that point, we were all shouting, like, 'Hey man, we got no fucking money and we're stuck! What the fuck!' So then he goes, 'Well, look, there's a guy from the county here, and I've worked it out with him that if you guys come down here tomorrow and clean up the trash, he'll give you gas money to get home'.

"So the whole band went back the next day to this huge 20,000-seater amphitheatre, and in 120-degree heat, we cleaned up all the garbage with trash barrels, before finally being given a total of $100 to get home. Everybody else in the band was depressed and pissed-off, screaming and yelling. But Jimmy and I got some comedy mileage out of it.

"That was one of the great things about that man. We were like, 'Well, yeah, this sucks. This is fucked-up. But you know what? It's just a little kink in the armour. We plan to make our fucking mark in the world here. You just sit back and watch us…'"

Above: A visit to Mom's place in Oregon, 1978
Opposite: Tearing it up at The Mustang Ranch. Walter: "This was taken in 1979, and that's the same Strat that's on the cover of all my CDs. My arm wore the finish off the guitar through so much playing. I believe the reason it turned yellow was from all the nicotine in the clubs. It just shows what all that touring and playing will do for it, y'know?"

NOTHIN' BUT THE BLUES

Blame John Travolta. As Walter remembers it, the Hollywood newcomer's breakout roles in first 1977's Saturday Night Fever, then 1980's Urban Cowboy, made the turn of the decade untenable for bands at the circuit's sharp end: "Those movies destroyed music for working musicians in the States for a while. They fucked up the scene. First, he did Saturday Night Fever, and guys couldn't get gigs because it was all disco. Then, three years later, he did Urban Cowboy. Now you could get gigs, but you had to wear cowboy boots, dance around and play Cotton-Eyed Joe. It was sickening."

By 1978, Walter was tired of playing cowboys. "Midnight Angel had done five nights a week at The Mustang Ranch," he says. "Five sets a night, for two years, without a break. But I was getting sick of it. One day, a friend of mine, Brandt Bindley, told me, 'Hey man, last Sunday I went to the Redondo Beach Pier and there was a bunch of older black guys playing blues at this little club'. They'd told him that if he brought me up there on a Sunday, I could play a song with them.

"So that Sunday, we went to the Redondo Beach Pier, to a little club called the Starboard Attitude, which is still there. We walked in, and these guys said, 'OK, he can play one song with us'. So I got up, played the song, and they said, 'Hey, play another song'. So I played another and they said to finish the set. When I finished the set, they asked if I wanted to join the band."

Walter sensed this was not just another rag-bag collective of LA also-rans, and so it proved: "The lineup was basically John Lee Hooker and Big Mama Thornton's backup band. The bandleader and organ player was Deacon Jones, who I love and who still plays on all my solo records. That guy was with Freddie King for fifteen years. He was with Curtis Mayfield and The Impressions when he was just a kid. He's the real thing. Then there was Finis Tasby, and the rhythm guitar player was Evans Walker.

"They were called the Coast To Coast Blues Band, but that was just a little club gig they did on weekends, minus John Lee Hooker. These guys were the guns-for-hire for the blues artists in LA. The bedrock of the whole thing was Deacon and Finis, then there were various other players they'd call when big blues guys were coming through LA and needed a backing band.

"So all of a sudden, I was in. I have a promo shot of that band where we're standing on a locomotive. It's easy to pick me out: I'm the only white guy and the only guy under fifty. Their nickname for me was 'nigger'. It wasn't looked down on. Maybe those were different days, but we'd be playing and Finis would look over and go, 'Hey, nigger!', and that meant to play a solo."

Open a blues encyclopedia at random. Bring your finger arbitrarily down onto any page and in all likelihood, you'll be pointing at a long-dead US heavyweight backed by Walter at the tail-end of the 1970s. "In that band, we played with Big Mama Thornton, John Lee Hooker, Pee Wee Crayton, Percy Mayfield, Lowell Fulson, Joe Tex.

"All that stuff I did, I did it through those guys. So I was both intimidated and elated. Sure, it was great to go to Midnight Angel and say, 'I'm through'. But I went from playing at a trendy club in Costa Mesa for a bunch of rich, coke-fuelled hipsters… to these guys."

Opposite: All aboard with the Coast To Coast Blues Band, 1979

Today, the names of those venerable performers seem auspicious, but with many of them scratching a living in the late-1970s, Walter's latest gig was anything but glamorous. As he recalls, it led him into a California that doesn't appear in any glossy holiday brochure and onto a dog-eat-dog circuit where a successful gig meant making it out alive: "We did not do shows for white audiences.

"I suddenly found myself playing in Compton, Watts, Inglewood, and going into all these areas of Los Angeles where white people just did not set foot. I remember, one Saturday night in downtown Watts, the band said to me, 'Hey man, here's $20, walk down to the liquor store on the corner and get us a bottle'. At which point, I said, 'I'm not doing it. I'm not walking through town, on my own, unaccompanied. I'm sorry, but I'm not gonna do that'.

"I had my pocket picked a couple of times. I even had a gun pulled on me at one club in Watts. I was on the stage, setting up my stuff, getting ready to play, and this guy walked up and pulled a gun, like, 'What the hell are you doing here, motherfucker?' At which point, everybody in the place grabbed him and threw him out, because I think they actually appreciated that I was there.

"They liked my playing. I became known to them, and some of the club owners sort of adopted me as this young white kid that could play the guitar. I was always incredibly respectful to everyone. I knew that I had to maintain a certain demeanour, or I would be in big trouble, physically."

For all the occupational hazards, a place on the stage of the hallowed John Lee Hooker was ostensibly a dizzy thrill for any young, blues-obsessed gunslinger. The man in the Stetson and shades, by any measure, was a stone-cold galactico of the genre, his groove-led hits through the '40s, '50s and '60s taking in benchmarks like Boogie Chillen, I'm In The Mood and Boom Boom.

And yet, as Walter explains, Hooker's undoubted genius didn't always make him an easy day-to-day band mate: "I still have deep, ultimate respect for his contribution to American music, and I'm in his debt for allowing me to do those shows. It was like going to a university. We just didn't groove on a personal level, whereas me, Deacon and Finis remain as close as brothers.

"It was partly that I was star-struck. Way down inside of me, I was feeling like I wasn't worthy of being there. For years, I'd been my own worst critic and worst enemy, feeling that I didn't deserve

I even had a gun pulled on me at one club in Watts. I was on the stage, setting up my stuff, getting ready to play, and this guy walked up and pulled a gun, like, 'What the hell are you doing here, motherfucker?' At which point, everybody in the place grabbed him and threw him out, because I think they actually appreciated that I was there. They liked my playing.

any accolade; that other guys were so much better and I was struggling just to get through this shit. Plus, I always had a hard time talking to the Hook. He had a stutter, and his voice was about four octaves lower than the normal human speaking voice. I didn't have a clue what he was saying. It might as well have been Esperanto.

"The first show I ever played with the Hook, we didn't even rehearse. I show up at the club and I say, 'Well, what are we gonna play?' Deacon goes, 'Every song, you just play an E chord. If we play a boogie, that's A, but other than that,

just play E. Here's an example. They call it stormy Monday – E! But Tuesday's just as bad – E! Lord and Wednesday's worse – E! And Thursday's all so sad – E!' So I say, 'OK, I got it, just play E'. Then Deacon says, 'And when he looks at you, play a solo, until he looks at you again, then you stop'.

"But here's the clincher. I'm not getting along with the Hook so good, and one day, I say to him, 'Hey man, I've done four or five shows with you now and we've never played One Bourbon, One Scotch, One Beer. It's your most famous song, and it was a big radio hit for George Thorogood here in the States. How comes we're not doing it?'

"At which point, the Hook walks out of the room with his head down, and Deacon goes: 'You really want to know why we're not doing that song? It's because the Hook don't think you can follow the changes'. I was dumbfounded! That one killed me."

From mute indifference, Walter remembers that his relationship with Hooker degenerated into nose-to-nose warfare: "We did a two-night run at the Belly Up club in San Diego, where I still play. That gig, I kept waiting to play a solo. I was the lead player: that was my gig. The Hook played guitar, I played guitar, so there were two guitar players up there and normally he'd give me a solo pretty much every song.

"That night, by about the fourth song, he still hadn't, until finally he looked over and pointed. By then, I had four songs' worth of bottled-up energy inside me, and I'm a pretty energetic player anyway, so I went right to the front of the stage and got completely lost in my solo, did the whole arm-in-the-air and this kind of shit, finished with a big flourish, bowed to the crowd and got a standing ovation.

"That was the only solo I played all night, and when we came off, the Hook's comment to me was, 'Hey, are you trying to steal my show?' I'm like, 'No, I'm not trying to steal your show. You hired me to play a fucking guitar solo. You want me to play like shit? You want me to detune first…?'"

Likewise, while Walter has endless reverence for the catalogue of Big Mama Thornton, he'll admit the Hound Dog diva could be a tricky customer at shows of the same period. "This was near the end of her life, so instead of Big Mama, by then, she was small, emaciated Mama. She was very thin, from a combination of age and having led a hard life.

"She dressed in men's cowboy clothes with the big hat and boots – like Roy Rogers or something – and she was very cantankerous. She drank a lot, and whatever venue you were in, she would come out, sit down on a piano stool, take her cowboy hat off, put it down and say, 'We ain't playin' 'til somebody comes up here and puts some paper money in my hat'. So she's asking for tips. That's old-school, right?

"So I show up for our first gig with Big Mama. She's in the back, and she says to me, 'I don't want to hear no psychedelic shit. All you got to do is play like B.B. King. You do that, you'll be OK'. So at the show that first night – and this is one of the things she did that intimidated me – she pointed at me and said into the mic, 'Now the white boy's gonna try to play like B.B. King'. Maybe she was actually trying to make a joke, I don't know.

"One thing I remember about Big Mama was that on some nights, her dentures would make it difficult for her to play the harmonica and she would have to take them out.

"One night she stopped, pulled out the dentures and handed them to me, like, 'Do something with these'. So I stood there, and she's looking at me, with these dentures in her hand, and they're dripping. I'm thinking to myself, 'How bad do I want this gig?' And I decided, 'Actually, I do want this gig'.

"So I grabbed the dentures, put 'em on top of my Fender amp and the warmth dried them out. At that moment, I really wished someone had invented hand sanitiser. I just had to wipe my hand on my pants and get on with the show."

Time has changed Walter's perception of the gig: "My feeling at that point was

One thing I remember about Big Mama was that on some nights, her dentures would make it difficult for her to play the harmonica and she would have to take them out. One night she stopped, pulled out the dentures and handed them to me. So I grabbed the dentures, put 'em on top of my Fender amp and the warmth dried them out. At that moment, I really wished someone had invented hand sanitiser. I just had to wipe my hand on my pants and get on with the show.

that I wasn't appreciated in Big Mama's band. But a few years ago, I was watching a video of an old gig that I got from Deacon. She's giving me guitar solos and at the end of them, she's saying, 'Let's hear it for Walter on the guitar!' I watched that and I actually started crying. I thought, y'know, that maybe she actually liked what I was doing. It didn't even dawn on me."

In terms of kudos, the gun-for-hire years were a rung up from bar-band hackery, but as for remuneration, Walter remembers being left with the crumbs each night. "I never made any money with those guys. It was never a well-paid gig. I was making five times the money playing in Midnight Angel.

"With John Lee Hooker and Big Mama Thornton, we were mainly playing little clubs that weren't much bigger than my kitchen. Back then, blues in general was at an all-time low, and at those gigs, you didn't get a guaranteed fee.

"You went and you played, and then, at the end of the night, they might hand you something. If you even got $25, you were smiling. I can remember the Hook handing Deacon a $10 bill after one gig. He looked at the money and he said, 'John Lee Hooker, I got a little baby at home! He don't do nothin' but eat and shit – and they both costin' me money!'

"I had to find ways to subsidise my John Lee Hooker and Big Mama Thornton years. There's a harp player on the Life In The Jungle album named Felix Flanagan. Now, at the time, Felix was the millionaire owner of a firm that produced micrometers, which are the little things that engineers use to measure thousandths of an inch.

"So I worked for this guy, out of my house, painting micrometer knobs. He would turn up with huge cardboard boxes of these things and pay me five cents a knob. So when I got into Canned Heat in 1980, that was definitely a big step up…"

Above: Willie Mae "Big Mama" Thornton

OUTTA CONTROL

By 1980, Canned Heat was a rock 'n' roll institution down on its luck. Under the leadership of founding members Alan 'Blind Owl' Wilson and Bob 'The Bear' Hite, hits like 1968's On The Road Again and Going Up The Country had taken the Los Angeles band from hippie favourites to global stars. Two decades later, the name still resonated, but the lineup was unrecognisable. Wilson had committed suicide in 1970, and Hite would die of an overdose in 1981, leaving drummer Fito De La Parra as the sole original member. Worse, the shreds of the band were now managed, after a fashion, by a West Coast biker gang.

Nonetheless, for Walter Trout, who in 1980 was scraping $25 a night flanking blues veteran J.D. Nicholson, the chance to join a name-band with a generous salary outweighed any misgivings. "At the time," he says, "we were called J.D. Nicholson and the Soul Benders, and we had a residency at a club in Hermosa Beach called The Lighthouse. J.D. was this incredible 70-year-old black keyboard player who had played with a lot of the greats out of Chicago. Once again, I was the only white guy, and I also got to front the band because I could sing. So I'd play there two or three nights a week with J.D., then go off with Deacon and Finis when they had a gig with Lowell Fulson or whoever.

"I remember, this one night, a couple of rugged-looking fellas came in and listened to the band. At the end of the night, they bought me a drink, hung out, and said they played in Canned Heat. Next night, they came back with this huge biker fellow, sat me down and told me this was the manager of Canned Heat. They said, 'Look, we have a tour of Australia coming up, but Henry Vestine's been drinking too much and would you be interested…?'"

A couple of caveats: "First, they asked me if I was addicted to drugs and if I drank a lot. Then I had to go play with the band, sit in at one of their rehearsals. And that was the moment when Fito said

I was in, because as the only original member, Canned Heat was really his band. They promised me good pay, so all of a sudden, that was an incredible career move for me."

No kidding. Micrometers aside, the months preceding Canned Heat had seen Walter pinball between a string of desperate day jobs. "I did a lot of things just to survive. I was a cook. I was a veterinary assistant. Just before Canned Heat, I'd taken a day job at a warehouse in Costa Mesa, because my girlfriend and I were about to lose our apartment. They produced various things for the medical industry. My job was to count out ten plastic bags that said 'Hazardous Waste' on them, put them into a bigger bag, put those into a box. I'd do that for eight hours a day. I subsidised my pay by becoming the factory pot dealer, selling the workers all the weed I scored up in Watts."

Handing in his notice, remembers Walter, was faintly surreal for both sides: "Basically, I had to go in the warehouse and tell the owners, 'Hey guys, did you ever heard of that band Canned Heat? Well, I'm their new lead guitar player. So I need to work here another month, then I'm gonna go on tour to Australia'. They were looking at me, like, 'OK, yeah, sure, we believe you…'"

Before the tour came the trial-by-fire. Walter remembers his debut gig, on New

Year's Eve 1980, as an early hint of the mayhem to come. "We played this club in LA and the first thing that happened was the manager – this big biker – handed me a jar of cocaine. He said to me, 'Here, this is for you for the evening, have fun'. That's how it started in Canned Heat. So after having told me, 'Yeah, you're replacing this guy because he's too high', they then hand me a jug of drugs and start plying me with shots of Jack. So I was thinking to myself, 'And you canned Henry Vestine because he drank? What is this culture I'm joining here?'

"I think that first show went OK. I got so buzzed. I thought the coke enhanced my performance at the time, but it's an illusion. It's a big lie. It's bullshit. Looking back, there are some things I recorded with Canned Heat that I don't want to hear again, and one of the reasons for that is that we were too high on drugs and the playing sucks."

If Walter was momentarily baffled by the double-standards of life in Canned Heat, he had learnt to walk the tightrope by the time the band left for 1981's notorious tour of Australia. Onstage, the guitarist could patently cut it, with the Boogie Assault live album from Oz seeing him scrawl thrillingly across classics like On The Road Again and Amphetamine Annie.

Opposite: Canned Heat in 1984

Offstage, things got messy. "Canned Heat was turbulent, but it was really fun to start with. On that tour, we flew into Adelaide. I'd been drinking all the way, and taken a couple of Quaaludes, and when we landed, the band carried me off the airplane, put me down on the conveyor belt with the luggage and stood there watching me go around. I still know some of those guys and they love to tell that story. I have a joke when people ask me about Canned Heat, which is that I was there for four years and I can't remember any of it. In fact, I'm surprised at how much I do remember."

With the band's musclebound management on hand in Australia, the musicians were free to raise hell with impunity. "When you were in Canned Heat," explains Walter, "you were the bikers' sort of pet project. Not only did

Canned Heat was turbulent, but it was really fun to start with. On that tour, we flew into Adelaide. I'd been drinking all the way, and taken a couple of Quaaludes, and when we landed, the band carried me off the airplane, put me down on the conveyor belt with the luggage and stood there watching me go around.

they manage the band, but they pretty much owned the band. We used to go to their clubhouses in the States, and we were always taken good care of."

On the flipside, woe betide anyone who crossed them: "I remember, one night in Australia, we were having a party, up there with all the bikers and the wild women, on the twelfth floor of this high-rise hotel. Now, these bikers all hated the promoter. They *despised* him. That night, the promoter was drunk, banging on the door and shouting, 'I booked this band, let me in!' He busted in, and promptly, a couple of the motorcycle guys grabbed him. Now, this is a true story. One guy grabbed one foot, another guy grabbed the other foot. They hung him over the balcony upside down from the twelfth floor. They had him by the feet; his arms were flapping and he was screaming.

"Then the head of the motorcycle club came out and said, 'Shut up!' When the promoter had stopped screaming, the guy said to him, 'You have two options here. You're either gonna leave through the door of the room or I'm gonna tell the brothers to drop you – but you're not staying at this party. So you let us know what you want'. The promoter screamed, 'Let me out the front door!' So they let him back up and he never tried to get in again."

As for Walter, his tastes tended more towards sex than violence: "There were insane amounts of women in Australia. A whole line of girls waiting outside the door to fuck me. These were the days before AIDS. One that stands out was an exotic dancer named Gypsy Fire. She had been Bob Dylan's mistress for a while. She came up to me at one gig and told me, 'I'm from the Planet Orgasm', at which point, we went off to erotic wonderland together. When I found out she had been Dylan's mistress, I felt like I was going into some sacred territory when I climbed in there.

"The whole situation in Australia was insanely incestuous. The funny thing is, that promoter had been having an affair with Fito's fiancée, who was this Australian girl. The promoter had a beautiful girlfriend himself, and in the middle of that tour he went back to his office in Sydney for a couple of days – and by the time he got back, his girlfriend had moved in with me. So he was pissed and yelling at me that I had stolen his girlfriend, while I was yelling at him that he had fucked Fito's fiancée. He was really in no position to moralise with me for stealing his girlfriend."

A party this hard couldn't last forever. Back in the States, long periods of inactivity left Walter kicking his heels and counting the pennies. The boxes of micrometers returned. The guitarist grew frustrated: "This was supposed to be a world-famous band and we just weren't working. I kept saying to the management, 'When are we gonna work? I want to be a guitar player here!'

"Finally, I called and told them, 'Look, I can't do this anymore. I'm in a famous band, but I'm broke. I'm gonna have to do something else'. The guy said, 'OK, meet me at the liquor store in Redondo Beach'. I sat there in my car and he pulled up next to me. I rolled my window down and he threw a giant plastic bag full of Quaaludes into my car and said, 'Go sell those.'"

Opposite and above: Let the good times roll. Backstage madness with Canned Heat in 1983 and 1984

It wasn't quite what Walter had in mind. Nor was Canned Heat's latest project-in-progress. In the early-1980s, rather than record a traditional studio album, the band's biker club management were pursuing the idea of a Beatles-style film, starring the band, associates and hangers-on. "We went through this phase where management decided this movie was going to make the band huge," explains Walter. "It's gonna be the Canned Heat version of A Hard Day's Night. It's gonna be produced by management, and they supposedly have Japanese financiers to back it, and it's really gonna make the band happen.

"Finally, I get the movie script in the mail. I actually still have it: even through divorce and homelessness, I still haven't given it up. They'd hired some guy to write this script, and he's obviously sat around on methadrine coming up with this. Here's a typical scene: two biker astronauts fly to the moon in a hypodermic needle. Another scene: a biker walks into a bank, takes one look at the bank president in the business suit and pukes on his hand.

"Another scene: a biker finds himself this raunchy lady. She rips a tampon out of her pussy, hands it to him and he promptly has a dream where he's riding the used tampon like a Harley. He rides into the ocean, a giant shark starts circling. The guy jumps off the used tampon, the shark eats the giant used tampon – and promptly dies of toxic shock syndrome.

"So I read this script and I was outraged. The band had already recorded music for the film. I called up Fito and I told him, 'That's it, I'm leaving the band. I quit. I'm gone. I don't want anything to do with this video. I will not have my name in the video. Just tell them it's Henry Vestine on guitar on the soundtrack'. I told him: 'It's this script. It's the worst fucking thing I've ever seen. I want to work, man. I want to be a guitar player'."

Fito concurred. "So we have a band meeting and he goes, 'You know what, man? You're right. We gotta make a change. We gotta get rid of the

management'. So Fito calls up the motorcycle club fellows and he tells them we're firing them. To which, they tell us they need us all to come up to their office in Los Angeles and have a meeting. We go up to the office and we sit there as this

So then this biker fellow says to us, 'OK, here's the only way that you guys are gonna live. We're gonna go through with the video, because we know it's gonna make us a million bucks. Then, after we've filmed it, we will no longer have a business relationship. We'll keep the money and you guys can fuck off.

large biker fellow tells us, 'I'm going to personally murder each and every one of you. If I only get one or two, and then I get caught and put in prison, that's OK, because the rest of my bros will be behind

me to finish off the rest of you. And Walter, I blame this on you, so you're going first."

The band members revised their position: "So then this biker fellow says to us, 'OK, here's the only way that you guys are gonna live. We're gonna go through with the video, because we know it's gonna make us a million bucks. Then, after we've filmed it, we will no longer have a business relationship. We'll keep the money and you guys can fuck off.

"So the management set up the video. It was filmed at this remote ranch out in the mountains, and we were all sure, while we were driving there, that they were taking us up there to kill us. They'd changed the script around. Each guy in the band now had his own section. Fito was a coke dealer, and he goes onto this big yacht to sell some coke. My scene, I'm in bed with a Mexican whore. I get up, throw her the money, this big guy covered with tattoos – my bodyguard – comes in and escorts me out, then I get into a limo and drive off into the sunset. I didn't enjoy filming it much. It was kinda like, 'Am I gonna die after this?' Like, 'OK, Walter, your scene is done – bang'.

"Years later, I was playing in Coos Bay, Oregon, with my solo band, and one of the guys who had financed that film came walking into the club while I was playing. And I thought, 'This is it now. This is where I'm gonna get it'. I was really nervous. But he just walked up to me on the break and he shook my hand, and he said, 'I want you to know that whatever went down, all of us on our end knew that you were gonna go on and do something. And I want you to know that we're really proud of you, and we're really behind you, and we want to be friends'. Then he handed over a DVD of the film. So it does exist. It's called The Boogie Assault. I think my section is on YouTube."

Above: Boogie Assault – the movie!
Opposite: Born to be wild. Canned Heat promo shot from 1984

JUNKYARDS IN YOUR EYES

A telephone rings in the summer of 1985. Picking up, our thirty-something protagonist hears a familiar voice bearing fantastical news. On the line is John Mayall: benevolent dictator of the legendary Bluesbreakers, and headmaster of the finishing-school lineup that has seen stars including Eric Clapton, Peter Green and Mick Taylor graduate from its ranks since 1963. Having locked eyes with Walter from the sleeve of the Beano album in 1966, the godfather of British blues now dangled an offer the flailing guitarist could hardly refuse.

"It's still hard for me to describe the elation of being asked to join the Bluesbreakers," remembers Walter. "I knew that as far as being a sideman guitar player in the blues genre, it was the peak. You couldn't go any higher. Maybe B.B. King would be bigger, but if you got that gig, you'd just stand in the background playing chords. I knew I'd hit the pinnacle.

"At this point," he explains, "I was still basically homeless and sleeping on the floor at a house in Huntington Beach owned by Bill Ward of Black Sabbath. The house was always filled with broke itinerant musicians and the trick was to find an open space on the floor to sleep. My friend, Doug Hounsell, was the only one paying Bill rent, while Bill lived in the garage and was pawning his platinum albums to get living money.

"None of us had any money. At night, Doug would run a giant electrical extension cord out the door up over the telephone lines, across the alley, and into a laundry room of an apartment building. He had a little 13 inch black and white TV, which he would place on a box and we would sit around and watch it. He always brought the extension cord in at the end of the night. One night, he forgot. We were passed out on the couch, and suddenly the TV went flying out the door, bouncing down the alley! It turns out that a trash truck had come down the alley, caught the cable, and Dougie went off in a mad dash trying to catch the television.

"So there I was in a world-famous band, *still* sleeping on my buddy's floor. One day, Bill Ward asked me to start a band with him and Tim Bogert, of Vanilla Fudge, Cactus and Jeff Beck fame. We called ourselves Blue Thunder. We did old rock 'n' roll, old blues – all sorts of stuff. It was great to hear Bill Ward play these styles of music he never got to explore with Black Sabbath, and he nailed it every night. But then John Mayall said to me: 'It's Blue Thunder or the Bluesbreakers'. So it was bye-bye Blue Thunder for me!"

Becoming a paid-and-credited Bluesbreaker was certainly a schoolboy fantasy, though as Walter explains, it wasn't quite a bolt from the blue. "In Canned Heat, we had done three shows opening for John Mayall back in 1982, when he put the original Bluesbreakers back together with John McVie, Mick Taylor and Colin Allen.

"We'd played three big club shows in Santa Cruz, Berkeley and San Francisco, where I started hanging out with John. He listened to me the first night and came up after to tell me he loved the way I played. That was our initial meeting and we hit it off greatly."

After-hours, liquor greased the wheels with Mayall's foot-soldiers. "That first night, we were all in the same motel. I was walking back from somewhere after the gig and there was John McVie and Mick Taylor, sitting on the stairs outside the motel with a bottle of rubbing alcohol and a bottle of orange juice, mixing drinks.

"So my way of breaking the ice was to say, 'Hey guys, my name's Walter and I play with Canned Heat. So how come you're drinking rubbing alcohol?' And John McVie – who by this point had the Rumours album out and was a multi-millionaire – said, 'Because it's 89 cents a bottle'. I said, 'Well, look, guys, I have a fifth of really good vodka, a cassette deck and a bunch of old blues tapes in my room. You guys wanna come up?' So off we go. The bass player from Canned Heat,

Ernie Rodriguez, he comes in there too, and we all sat around drinking my vodka and playing my blues tapes, having a great visit.

"Then John McVie passed out on the floor of my room. We couldn't even wake him to give him another drink. And this is a true story: when one of the tapes ended, I went over to the cassette player and said to the guys in the room, 'What do you want to hear next?' At which point, John McVie's head came up off the floor, his eyes opened and he said, 'Please, no Stevie Nicks!' Then he went back down onto the floor."

The run came to an end. "But after those three shows, John asked, 'What are you doing now?' Well, Canned Heat wasn't doing much. So he said, 'I'd love to hear you playing guitar with Mick Taylor. Why don't you come and do a few shows

with me?' So suddenly, I was off playing rhythm guitar for Mick Taylor at four or five shows in California as a member of the original Bluesbreakers. John Mayall would feature me every night, and I would even sing Dust My Broom. That was just a killer experience."

Even as he pinched himself, Walter's giddy excitement was tainted by deep insecurity. "When they were making those classic Bluesbreakers albums, I was in high school. Those records were a huge part of my youth. I learned to play guitar by listening to those records and imitating them. So this was like being invited to join the Stones.

"At the start of the Bluesbreakers, I used to think to myself, 'What am I even doing here? I'm just this scared, frightened, fucked-up individual from a little town in New Jersey, and now I'm in

John Mayall's band'. I just couldn't put it together. I didn't feel like I deserved it. I felt like I was gonna wake up the next day and it would all be a dream, and I would still be scrambling to play a bar in Jersey and make ten bucks. It was kinda like, 'Am I fooling these people?' I just never felt like I was that good.

"I can still remember, the first time I played with the original Bluesbreakers in California, I was sitting backstage and I just kept going, 'This is such an honour, I can't believe it'. Finally, Mick Taylor jumped up and said, 'Will you stop with the fucking *honour*? If John didn't think you could play, you wouldn't be here. We think you play fucking great, so quit telling us what a fucking honour this is'. It almost embarrassed them."

Walter duly detonated the shows, making it even more of a wrench to return to the opiated car-crash of Canned Heat while the Bluesbreakers rolled on down the road. That might have been that. And yet, as the guitarist recalls, the short-term contracts from Mayall kept coming. "The first tour I actually went on with John was in 1983. He'd hired Canned Heat as his band, so we went out and toured America and Canada as Canned Heat with John Mayall. We would do our set, then bring John on and do another hour with him."

Soft-spoken and steely, Mayall was never caricatured by the music press as a hellraiser – indeed, he had famously canned Mick Fleetwood from the Bluesbreakers in 1967 for drunkenness – but Walter paints that tour as a protracted drinking session: "Of all the years I played with John, it was just that one Canned Heat tour that he was drinking on. At the end, he went to AA and stopped everything. But on that tour in 1983, he and I bonded over getting fucked-up. We'd drink anything, at any time, and we didn't care.

"At the end of the night, we'd take all the half-finished drinks from the club and pour them into this wine bottle that John had printed a label for. It was called Chateau Hibiscus. He'd cork it, and next day we'd sit in the back of the van and do the ceremony of uncorking the Hibiscus

and checking the bouquet: 'Yeah, it smells like there's a little Jack Daniel's in there, mixed with Budweiser, topped off with Pernod…' We'd have little cups back there, so we'd sample it and discuss what was the overwhelming flavour of that batch.

"Even then, John was never wild and crazy. Even when he was drunk, he was very businesslike, and the show and tour were always of the utmost importance. He was incredibly wasted – as was I – but he was able to hold it better than me. He never got really sloppy, and he could maintain the British stiff-upper-lip thing, while I was just walking around puking on my shoes."

Having proved his mettle on the road – as both musician and drinker – Walter now found himself cordially invited into the Brain Damage Club: a near-mythical, semi-formal circle of celebrity lushes who convened in the replica of a British pub that Mayall had built in his LA home. "John would appoint you a member of this club," explains Walter, "and the criteria was that you had to have drunk enough in your life, or taken enough drugs, to display sufficient brain damage.

"There were famous movie actors in the club, porno stars, lots of musicians. I was the first – and, I believe, the only – member of Canned Heat who became a member. You actually got a membership card, and you'd get a newsletter in the mail when the Brain Damage Club was going to meet, and all that meant was that people would go to John's bar and get shit-faced. This pub even had a tree planted in the middle that he'd gone out and cut down. Of course, after John sobered up, the Brain Damage Club closed. He didn't want people coming to his house and getting shit-faced drunk at that point."

Backstory complete, we return to the fateful phone-call of 1985. "So John called me up," explains Walter, "and he said, 'I have a tour of Europe booked. Come do the tour, we'll see how it goes, and if you do well, you're in the band'. The lineup at the time was Joe Yuele on drums, Bobby Haynes on bass, and me

and Coco Montoya on guitar. The thing was that Coco played the guitar left-handed, upside-down, as did Albert King. Which meant that he took a right-handed guitar and just turned it over; he didn't change the strings backwards. In the Mayall band, that always used to freak people out, because if I broke a string during a solo, Coco would take his guitar off and hand it to me, and I'd turn it over and keep playing. I'd do the same for him.

"So my first show with the Bluesbreakers is Bratislava, Czechoslovakia, at this huge outdoor amphitheatre. This is the first time the band has ever met me and of course it's like, 'Who's the new guy?' Well, I started drinking at the venue, and before the show I was going around trying to find cocaine. This is behind the iron curtain, when it was part of the USSR. So I keep on asking these roadies, 'Where can I get some coke, man?' and they're looking at me, like, 'It doesn't exist here, and if you get caught with that shit here, you're in a Russian Gulag for the rest of your life'.

"So I'm getting more and more drunk, and more and more pissed, until finally, we're onstage, and I couldn't even stand up. This is the first show and the band is looking at me like, 'What the fuck?' I'm yelling at the monitor guy, 'Give me some fucking blow, man!' I remember, John was on the mic, and I took my string-winder and I stuffed it up my nose, walked up to him, stood right in front of him and started turning it in my nose."

He wasn't finished: "At the end of the night, I was hanging out of the window of my hotel in the centre of Bratislava, throwing up and screaming at the people on the town square, 'Where the fuck is Mozart when you need him?' John and Bobby tried to talk me down because I was just losing it. At that point, all three members of the band told John, 'You've gotta get rid of this dude. This guy is out of his fucking mind.'"

Opposite: Mick Taylor, Walter and John McVie on the infamous rubbing alcohol day

Mayall declined to drop the axe, even as Walter upped the ante. "Next night, we went to Berlin to play the Quasimodo. It was my first time in Berlin, but the club was only a block away so I told the band, 'Yeah, I'm gonna walk to the gig'. So I went out walking around Berlin, went into some bars, started drinking beers and got rip-roaring shit-faced. I was completely lost, and I couldn't even remember the name of the club, so I couldn't ask anybody.

"I was just stumbling around downtown Berlin. I went into an alley and was leaning against this building weeping, when this car pulled up and it was this lady who was the manager of the Quasimodo. She got me to the club and I made it in time for the last two songs. By which point, the band were saying to John, once again, 'What are you doing with this idiot?'

"But John did not get rid of me. He kept me in there. That's one of the reasons I love the guy. He stuck with me in the face of all this shit. I've asked him

about this a lot over the years. I say to him, 'In my band, I wouldn't put up with anyone doing the stuff I did back then. Why did *you* put up with it?' John has always given me the same answer. He says, 'Number one, no matter how fucked-up you got, you always seemed to be able to play…'"

Against all logic and reason, Mayall was right: however dire Walter's personal condition, he was always able to conjure magic when a Stratocaster was placed in his hands. On the stage, live releases like 1987's The Power Of The Blues gave hard evidence of a player whose feel and fire jostled even his feted predecessors off their pedestals, and in the studio, he was often touched by genius. "My own favourite moment from the Bluesbreakers is One Life To Live," says Walter of the highlight from 1988's Chicago Line. "I remember John gave me a four or five-chorus solo and it just came out really good. The song is based on this very dark lick that John plays, and I remember that Coco didn't know what to do with the

solo. I said, 'Hey, I know what to play'. So we played it once, and that, out of my whole career, is one of my very best."

Mayall had a second reason for keeping Walter on the payroll. "He always says there was a certain humour to my behaviour. Y'know, I figure it entertained him. He was sober now, so he was living vicariously through this maniac. There were many nights where the band would carry me to my hotel room and lay me down on the bed while I lay there and threw up. One night, John came in my room and recorded me throwing up for forty minutes, then went home and overdubbed Kraftwerk behind the vomiting. Next day, he gave me this tape with me puking and this weird synth music behind it."

Spend a night on the next barstool and there *was* a certain humour to Walter's madcap antics of the mid-1980s. Spend a little longer in his company, and you realised this was a tragic figure, anaesthetising himself against his torrid past and unravelling in real-time.

The nights grew longer, the mornings darker. From boyish dabbles back at Collingswood, the drink and drugs had spiraled to a joyless daily ingestion. Walter, by his own admission, was in freefall.

Addicts speak of rock bottom, and in 1986, it took the form of an episode in Canada equal parts desperate and demeaning. "This was one of the big wake-up calls about my addiction," recalls Walter. "We'd just played the Vancouver World's Fair, and after the gig, there was me and this old musician who was playing with Albert Collins. I don't want to besmirch the man's rep, so I won't say his name, but he said he could get us some coke.

"So I give him the money and he takes off. At 5am, I'm still waiting in my room and I'm drunker than shit. Finally, there's a knock and there he is with the coke. Now, the plan is, we're gonna cook it and make what's called freebase, which is a higher version of crack. This ain't light. It's not Coke Zero. It's fully loaded. I had

a glass pipe and a blowtorch, and we've got ammonia: we're like a couple of chemists. He goes: 'Well, we need a coffee filter to filter it through'. Well, fuck, I didn't travel with coffee filters. So he goes, 'OK, let's use some underpants'.

"So I went through my suitcase and I got out the cleanest dirty pair of underpants I could find. Jockey shorts. We stretched them out, and we used that as a filter. We poured the shit through, then it dried out, and what you do is, all the shit goes through the filter, and what's left on the top, you scrape it off and smoke it. So we've got the glass pipe, and we're scraping the yellow-brown cocaine base that we've made into the pipe, and we're taking turns.

"We run out of the coke, but there's still stains all over the underwear, so now we're cutting little squares out of the underpants, and we really don't know or care if the stain is actual cocaine residue or piss and shit. We're actually fighting over this, like, 'I want that stain there, God damn it!'

"Finally, he left, and about two hours later, I was sitting in my room sorta vibrating when Mayall calls and tells me it's time to go get the airplane. I stood up, looked in the mirror and said to myself, 'I am from good genetic stock. My mother was a classy, brilliant, learned, great lady. I'm a direct descendant of James Fennimore Cooper, I'm sort of my mom's golden child and I had all this potential'. But there I was. I'd just been in my hotel room with this old guy, smoking my underpants through a glass pipe. That was a huge wake-up call. That really made me start thinking about what I was doing to myself. Like, 'What has fucking happened to me…?'"

Opposite: The Bluesbreakers, 1985
Above: The Bluesbreakers with B.B. King. Walter: "I believe that's the first time I met B.B. King, with Mayall, Charlie Musselwhite, Coco Montoya and Deacon Jones, at the Beacon Theater in New York. B.B. King is even nicer than everyone says he is. He's the finest, most unassuming human being that you will ever meet."

TO BEGIN AGAIN

July 9th, 1987. The history books shrug their shoulders, having little of consequence to report on that date. Walter Trout remembers it as his first day free of drink and drugs, and by extension, his rebirth. Even post-underpants, shaking the insidious habits of two decades had taken a run-up. Traditional twelve-step meetings had been attempted in Newport Beach, and rejected when fellow addicts began pestering the star in their midst for autographs: "One guy – I felt bad for him – told me his mom was in the hospital dying and would I take my guitar in and sing to her? I was going there to get away from pressures and demands and not have more put on me. I was trying to deal with my own crap. I never went back after that."

More instrumental, says Walter, was the backing of Mayall – perhaps realising his charge had sailed beyond comical scrapes – and the badgering of Little Feat's Richie Hayward. "John was like a dad to me, and Richie would be saying, 'You need to check yourself out. You're gonna feel better, you're gonna play better. Are you really having fun being all loaded like this…?'"

Another hand that helped pull Walter from the mire was that of Carlos Santana, who urged the guitarist to stop sabotaging his congenital talent after witnessing a train-wreck show in Berlin. "I was on the stage, playing sloppy, being a buffoon," he recalls. "Santana spent a few days slapping me around and handed over a book called Discover Your Possibilities. He said, 'Look, there's religion in here, and you can take or leave that, but there's a lot of psychology too'. The gist was that everyone has been given a gift, and by making the most of your abilities and sharing them, you can make the world a better place."

If sobriety would have been unthinkable to Walter's frazzled counterpart of the early-1980s, his first clear-headed moves seemed equally out of character. Marriage to long-term girlfriend Donna Larson was one thing; quitting the band he had worshipped as

a teenager quite another. "One of the proudest moments of my life," he says, "is being hired by the Bluesbreakers. I never took it for granted. I never got blasé about standing in that spot. That band was Mount Everest. What better gig was there for a guy like me?

"If I hadn't gotten sober, I would probably still be in Mayall's band, because I didn't have the guts to make the move. But getting sober gave me a bit of courage. I remember the night I quit the Bluesbreakers. It was March 6th, 1989 – my 38th birthday – and we were playing in Gothenburg, Sweden.

"I was up there on the stage, in this big, beautiful symphony orchestra hall. I was playing in this great band, touring the world, making great money. I'd sobered up, and things were starting to come into better perspective for me.

"I knew I was on the cusp of some big changes. When I came out to California in 1974, it was my dream to have my own band, but then I started getting these gigs as a sideman. I was up there on the stage in Gothenburg, thinking, 'I need to take a chance now'.

"I was 38, and by that age, most guys are trying to get into the second or third phase of their solo career. There are other guys who've never gone the sideman route. Y'know, Joe Bonamassa

has never been a sideman. Whereas with me, it was always, 'You need a guitar player in LA, you call Walter Trout'. Like the almost-nameless backup guy."

As the band performed, the cogs turned: "While I was playing this gig, I kept thinking and thinking, and finally, I decided, 'I'm gone. I'm done. I've made my decision and I've gotta go for this now'. Right after the show, I went to John's room and told him I was gonna leave the band. I started crying. John started crying. He told me I was just emotional because it was my birthday and I'd feel different tomorrow. I said, 'No, I'm serious here. This is it'.

"Finally, John said OK. But he told me, 'Of course I'll support you, and best of luck to you, but you need to realise that if you quit the band, and you go out and take the gamble on a solo career, then six months down the line you think you've made a mistake, don't call me and say you want your gig back, because by then, I will have gotten another player. Once you're gone, you're gone. Once you leave here, coming back is not an option.'"

Opposite: Newly sober, Walter cools down at the Bluesbreakers aftershow with a glass of water, 1987

The ultimatum was terrifying, but Walter had irons in the fire. "There had been one night in Denmark, a week or two before I quit, when Mayall got the flu and was incredibly sick. The promoter, Thomas Helweg, said, 'Look, if you cancel this show, I'm gonna lose so much money'. My idea was for the Bluesbreakers to go on without John, and at the end of the night, I'd tell the audience that if anyone thinks they didn't get a good show, I'd give them their money back.

"So that night, John stayed at the hotel, and Coco and I took turns fronting the Bluesbreakers, doing stuff we never usually did. I remember us doing Hey Joe, Red House, Foxy Lady, Crossroads, Spoonful, some Stones stuff. We played for three hours, went down great, and when we got off the stage, a guy came up and told me he was from the Bozz Of Electra label in Denmark and that he'd offer me the chance to make my own record. Then the

promoter said, 'If you make his record, I'll book the tour'. So it was put right in my lap."

Likewise, the solo lineup was right under Walter's nose: "I had this little bar band in Huntington Beach. I would play with these guys five nights a week at this bar called Perqs whenever I was home. I basically called them up from Sweden and said, 'We're gonna go into the studio in Stockholm and make a record'. So that little bar band of mine became the Walter Trout Band. We recorded my debut album in Stockholm – and it just killed."

Life In The Jungle was both a new dawn and a nod to the past, with Walter's compadre Jimmy Trapp drafted on bass, and the album's originals drawn from the guitarist's stockpile. "We mainly did old songs of mine on that first album," he explains. "I kinda had a backlog of stuff. The Mountain Song, I'd written when I was about 19. But I had been put off songwriting for a while.

When I first moved to LA, I had the opportunity to play for this big-time record producer. He said to me, 'You play great, you sing great, but your songs suck. Go home, write ten good songs – then maybe I'll talk to you'.

"That stopped me writing songs for a while. But then, when I was in Mayall's band, I wrote the title song Life In The Jungle. And it's a true story: a friend had come to see the band at Perqs one night. She walked home and got murdered in front of her house, just three blocks away. When I heard she got killed, I got so upset. I couldn't sleep, so I went out, walking around town at a rapid pace. I suddenly looked up and I was in front of her house, where she'd been stabbed to death at her front door. So in that song, the jungle is the city."

Opposite: Promo shot by Donna Trout, 1989
Above: Recording Life In The Jungle in front of 63,000 people at the Midtfyns Festival, July 2, 1989

Opposite (clockwise from top left):
Getting up close and personal with the crowd in Helsingor, on the first Tour of Denmark in 1989

Playing a very intimate venue (or possibly even somebody's living room!) Denmark, 1989

A lot of hot air. Having a laugh about amusing Danish place names

Above: We have posters! Mongo and Walter by a 1989 Danish Tour poster

Left: The love affair with Denmark begins, 1989

The Jungle sessions were a wham-bam thrill-ride, and when tracking paused for an impromptu festival set on July 2nd, 1989, the solo band proved themselves fist-tight on the stage. "We were right in the middle of making that first record," explains Walter, "when our promoter, Thomas Helweg, got us a gig at the Midtfyns Festival in Denmark. We had the slot right before the headliner, which was Little Feat. We were completely unknown. We didn't even have any roadies, so the audience watched these dirty, unshaven guys come out and set up all this equipment, and thought we were just the stage-hands.

"Then we put our instruments on, turned around, counted to four and proceeded to blow the doors off the place. We almost started a riot right there, in front of 63,000 people. They just freaked out. That night, Little Feat could not follow us. That gig happened to be recorded, so we took some live cuts from that and put those on the album. We even took some studio stuff off to get the live cuts on there, because they were just so exciting."

Released in 1989, Life In The Jungle could hardly hope to conquer the planet, given that it was only distributed in Scandinavia, but these spit-and-grit songs represented career vindication and thrilling proof that Walter could fly solo. "The album came out and we did great," he remembers, "but because it was on a small Danish label, it was only sold in Denmark, Norway and Sweden. I do remember there being a review in The Times in London, which said, 'There's good news and bad news. The good news is, this is the greatest album ever released in the blues-rock genre. The bad news is, does the blues-rock genre really need another album?' I could just take the first quote out of context and put it on marketing posters."

The Scandinavian market was less sniffy: "It went great for us when we first came out there. We sorta became the house band of Denmark. Dan Araco did all those first tours of Europe as the backline guy, and he'd also be my protector and fight for me physically if he had to, because he's a very big, muscular Italian guy. Right from the start, I had Phil Caseberry running the

sound in Europe. We'd go over there for six weeks at a stretch and play every night. You could drive from one end of the country to the other in four hours, so we'd hit every little bar and tavern. A lot of places we played were just tiny neighbourhood bars, but after that first record came out and we'd played that festival, we were a happening act, and wherever we played they were just freaking out.

"I have a video of us literally starting a riot at one gig. The funny thing was that the club owner had come out and said to me, 'The crowd is getting too wound up, so can you play some ballads?' Now, this is just me, but I hate being told what to do.

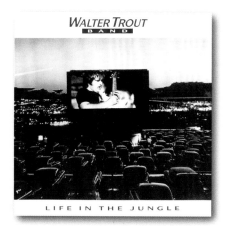

WALTER TROUT BAND

LIFE IN THE JUNGLE

So I remember saying, 'How's this?', then turning around and whipping into Long Tall Sally by Little Richard. One of the roadies had a film camera and he was behind us onstage, so you can see from the back as the audience almost attack the stage. All these big Danish guys get in front of the stage and lock their arms to form a human shield. There's this massive, free-for-all, chaotic riot going on, and we're just having a ball."

Post-Gothenburg, the stage was becoming the scene of regular epiphanies. As Walter stepped out to headline Denmark's Holstebro Jazz and Blues Festival on September 29th, 1990, he couldn't have suspected that somewhere in the melee was the woman who would steer his solo career, captivate his muse, salvage his finances, awaken his spirituality and save him from an addled early grave. Enter, then, Anne Marie Bech Brændgaard: a

Scandinavian advertising executive whose head-turning looks and quick wit belied her business acumen and nose for bullshit.

Twenty-four years later, Marie remembers that she almost skipped the show for a night in front of the TV: "I was just gonna sit in my apartment and do nothing that night. I was exhausted from a week at the office. Then a friend of mine, Freddy Petersen, came in and told me they were going to see Walter Trout play that night and did I want to go? I was so ready to say, 'Heck no, I'm not going anywhere tonight'. Then I just heard my voice say, 'Sure, I'll go'. From that moment on, I was just pulled in a direction that I didn't really understand."

For Walter, there's no question that a higher power was at work: "I'm headlining this music festival in this little town. There were 2000 people in this hall, but somehow I could see through the whole crowd of people to this blonde at the back of the room. She and I were just staring at each other. Then she started moving toward the stage, and this sounds like a movie, but it was like the Red Sea parting as the people moved aside. She stood in the front, and at one point I tried to walk sideways without losing her eye contact and fell over the mic stand. I signalled to her like crazy: 'Don't leave, I need to talk to you'.

"She stuck around until I came back out. We walked around this little Danish town that's a thousand years old, and after about forty minutes, I said, 'You're gonna move to America. We're gonna get married and have children. We're gonna get old together'. I told her, 'You don't even have a say in this, because this is fate. This is meant to be, and it's gonna happen whether you believe it or not'. She just looked at me and told me I was completely crazy."

Marie had already marked Walter's card as no-angel: "Oh, I knew he was a player. I could just tell. It was so obvious. Just the fact that when I got back there in the dressing room, all the guys were looking at me like, 'OK, so here's the next one'. Then Walter told me we were going to get married, and of course I thought he was out of his mind. You don't meet somebody and tell them you're going to grow old together within forty minutes."

Walter's romantic proclamation came with small-print. "After I'd said all that," he remembers, "I then had to explain that there was just one small problem, which was that I was already married. But I told Marie: 'I'll take care of that'. I called home and said, 'I'm bringing home a six-foot Danish blonde and I want a divorce'. Boom. I made it happen. About nine days later, Marie agreed that I was right. She had her own advertising agency, so she closed that, sold all the furniture and came to America. We'd only known each other a couple of weeks."

Over the years, Marie would inspire a starburst of Walter's greatest songs. Now, right out of the blocks, she breathed life into perhaps his most important one. "We did Prisoner Of A Dream in Copenhagen," recalls Walter of 1990's follow-up album. "We were pretty much done, and it was a good record, but we needed one more song. Well, I had this ballad. I wrote it the same day that I wrote The Mountain Song. I had come home and found Delphene with another guy. Instead of freaking out, I just said, 'You guys go

ahead and continue undulating', then I grabbed my Martin, ran outside and wrote The Love That We Once Knew as I stood on the railroad tracks.

"I'd had this ballad for years and never done anything with it. So we recorded that, and I think what gave the song its emotional power was that it was just a couple of days earlier that I told my current wife I had fallen in love with Marie and that I wanted a divorce. When I went into the studio to sing it, Marie came in

there with me, so I was looking at her while I was singing this song about, y'know, a couple being through."

The Love That We Once Knew proved to be the tipping-point, starting an imperious march up European single charts in 1990, scattering A-list pop behemoths like ninepins and exposing the market's chin for the Prisoner Of A Dream parent album. "That song ended up becoming this gigantic radio hit," remembers Walter. "Two weeks after that record came out, I met up with the record label in Copenhagen and they said, 'It's a massive hit! You're making so much money! We've never had a record do this well!'

"I was outselling everyone. The album went to #1 in Holland. I still have the chart. I'm there at #1, then there's Madonna, Bon Jovi, Bryan Adams. I played to 500,000 people at the Parkpop festival in The Hague. So we were kinda off and running at that point. It felt like, this is starting to go…"

Above: Marie and Walter, October 24, 1990

TAKE CARE OF YO' BU$INE$$

High times – but hold the champagne. As his early solo records hijacked the charts and fans scrummed hungrily at his stage barriers, Walter was nagged by the gulf between his apparently booming career and living conditions. "At that point," he recalls, "just to pay the rent, I was having to pawn my guitars every month. When Marie first moved in with me, we had a little one-room apartment. My mother had passed on and left me a little love seat and a 13-inch black-and-white television. We ate meals off plastic plates, sitting on the floor. We slept on a throwaway mattress. We had *nothing.*"

Something – or someone – didn't add up. No number-cruncher, Walter had so far buried his head, preferring blind faith to analysis of the books. Not so Marie. "I never made a dime at this career until she took over running it," he reflects. "Without Marie, I'd be dead or broke, or both. In those early solo years, I was ripped off for so much money, from various managers and labels, and she was the only one who was able to see it and bring it to my attention."

The sharks were circling from the start. "I remember the first manager I had when I went solo. We had a little tour of northern California booked, and when I tried to get paid from the venues, they kept saying, 'Oh yeah, we sent the money to your manager'. Near the end of the tour, when we didn't even have gas money, I called his mother and she told me he'd moved to Africa. He'd taken all the money and I never heard from him again.

"On Life In The Jungle, all the money was stolen by the German guy who negotiated the record deal. He'd sent me a contract in German, and I'd told him, 'Well, I want a deal, but I can't sign a fucking contract in a language I can't even read'. So he gave me what he said was a translation, and I signed it. Years later, when I had a German guy in my band – Martin Gerschwitz – I asked him to read the original contract, and it was completely different from the translation. I didn't make ten cents from that album.

"Next, six weeks after Prisoner Of A Dream came out – and this was my big hit record – I go see the record label at their offices in Copenhagen, thinking I'm gonna see how we're doing and get a cheque. The label was called Bozz Of Electra. It was not affiliated with Elektra Records in the US. And they're gone. The office is empty. They'd absconded with everything and disappeared, and to this day, I've never heard a word or received a cent."

The daylight robbery continued: "After Prisoner Of A Dream, I got approached by this big-time LA manager, and I went out and played a tour. Now, the way a tour works is, I make a certain gross, then I pay the band, the agents, the manager, and I get what's left at the end. So I did a ten-week tour, and at the end, this manager gave me $1,500. So I'd made $150 a week.

"Marie kept telling me, 'These guys are ripping you off'. But I was blind. I thought these were my friends. I was trusting and lacking business acumen. But Marie was not trusting and she did not lack business acumen. She's got insight like a knife. She's the one that, by actually looking at the accounts, proved how I was getting robbed in my early career. She had it right there in black-and-white, because I didn't believe it."

Smelling a rat, Marie swung into action: "She had started working side by side with me as my road manager after we got together. And now, unbeknownst to me, she got the set of books from our managers, listing that I had ended up

with $1,500. Then she called up our agent in London, who booked the entire tour, and asked him to send a copy of his books over. She didn't ask me, she just did this. I came back one day and she had both sets of books out, and she said, 'Take a look at this'. There was a discrepancy of tens of thousands of dollars. She proved it to me, showed me exactly how he did it. Just on that one tour, he had stolen a huge sum of money from me. I had a second manager at the time; he'd been presented with the fake set of accounts too and was just as surprised at the rip-off as we were.

"After Marie convinced me, and I realised there was more to her than just a beautiful blonde, we set up a hidden video camera in the bookshelf and asked this manager to come over for coffee. So we sat down, she laid out the books and said, 'What have you got to say for yourself?' He said, 'Yep, you got me. I've got the money. But it's all in a Mexican bank, so you're going to have to go down to Mexico, get a Mexican lawyer and sue me down there.'"

Diving down this legal rabbit-hole was an exhausting prospect. Walter shrugged his shoulders, took the hit and installed Marie as his manager and business head. "At that point, she said, 'Let me take over your career'. But we had to draw lines. Marie would say to me, 'Are you speaking to me as my boss? Because if you are, OK. But if you're speaking as my husband, fuck you'. Nobody wanted to be in the next hotel room to us, because we were either fighting or physically making up, and both of them were very loud.

"So it wasn't always smooth on the road. But Marie is responsible for any business success I might have had. From 1995's Breaking The Rules onwards, she's negotiated every record deal I've had. The music business is like a swimming pool full of great white sharks, and from that moment on, we dove in together and fought them off. I went back the next year, did the exact same tour – same venues, same guys, same tour bus – but this time, I brought home a lot of money comparatively."

Promo shot, 1990

Opposite: Studio shot, 1990
Above: 40th birthday celebrations with the obligatory stripper, March 6 1991

Business was looking up. Sobriety was a good fit. On September 28th, 1991, this one-time bed-hopping berserker embarked on the second marriage that flourishes to this day. "It's really one of those stories where two people are changed by each other," says Marie. "I think Walter got focus when we got together, and found a belief in something other than just the next town and the next gig. He suddenly had a bigger plan than just living in the moment. I think that's certainly kept him wanting to stay alive."

"It took me years and years to understand what love really is, and Marie showed me," agrees Walter. "I never felt any kind of commitment to another human being like I do to her, in a spiritual, deep way. From the moment we met, I felt a higher power, and you can call it whatever you want, but I have felt it work for me. The night I met her, after half an hour, I heard a voice say, 'You're looking at the mother of your children'. Through our life together, I've come to realise the depth of spirit that she and I share. It's an eternal bond. It's something that even after we're both dead, I know that we will still be souls together."

On a spiritual even keel, and with the nuts and bolts in safe hands, Walter was able to focus on the night-by-night detonation of the international blues circuit. "A few years back," he says, "I found a video of me playing Hey Joe in Holland at the start of my solo career. My energy is just unbelievable. When Marie watched it, she said, 'You were so full of adrenaline back then, you were almost bordering on insanity'. It's almost scary to watch."

The open-jawed consensus was that Walter's warp-speed, Strat-flaying runs were the most thrilling spectacle that blues-rock had to offer in the early-1990s. Not everyone agreed. Sniping from the shadows were the blues purists, whose perennial criticism of the bandleader's explosive guitar style would prompt the design of merch T-shirts

emblazoned with the knowing slogans 'Too Many Notes Too Loud' and '2 Blues 4 Rock – 2 Rock 4 Blues'.

As sideman in Mayall's venerable Bluesbreakers, the attacks had been deflected. Now, as a solo artist, Walter went nose-to-nose: "I remember going to play a blues festival in France, and half the audience walked out. It was full of snobs and purists saying, 'What is this shit? These guys are white! How can you say this is blues?' The next night, we went and played what was billed as a music festival, and because it didn't have that 'blues' label, they went nuts.

"I used to take it personally. Now I don't give a fuck. I want to say to these purists, 'You know what? I'm making a great living. I get people to my gigs. My records sell. If you don't like it, I don't give a shit'. Blues is actually an art form, and any art form needs to progress and change to reflect the times it exists in. Otherwise, you could say Picasso was bullshit because he wasn't painting like Michelangelo in the Renaissance.

"You can either be an artist who is secure in their vision, and just plough through the bullshit, or you can let yourself be intimidated by it. In which case, your attempts at art are invalid, because you're trying to tailor it to what you think somebody wants to hear.

"Anyway, I think a lot of that is changing now. The purists are sorta dying off. Nobody really gives a shit anymore what they have to say. If you go to a blues festival in the States, it's 98 percent guys that look like me. It's the same with people who 'Like' my Facebook page: white guys between the age of 45 and 65. I hate to use the word, but it's a certain demographic. Blues has become their music now. So that kinda kicks the purists in the ass."

Opposite: Walter and Marie tie the knot, September 28th, 1991. Walter: "That was the best day of my life, apart from the birth of my sons. I mean, look at me. That's not a fake smile. I was head-over-heels in love there. Still am."
Above: The only existing shot of Walter with a wedding ring, 1991

Promo shot, 1991

Walter and Jimmy doing their thing, Holland, 1991
Walter: "That was my wife's attempt to spiff up our image.
Jimmy is wearing a $300 hat. But the owner of Provogue
took it – so that was the end of Jimmy looking spiffy."

Unlike the blues-rock automatons slavishly following the prescribed twelve-bar format, musical evolution was much on Walter's mind as his solo career gathered pace. As such, in 1992, Transition was an apt title for his third album, even if in hindsight, this was a musical blind alley he deeply regretted turning down. "That album hurt my career," he reflects. "It was a setback."

From the start of Transition, remembers Walter, bad omens jostled around him. "There are a couple of bands I've heard in my life that I despise. One time, I had an aspiring girlfriend who was a big fan of REO Speedwagon. I told her I wouldn't allow any record by that band into my house, and that was the end of that. So who do my management – this is before Marie took over – now hook me up with to produce Transition? That's right: the guy who produced REO Speedwagon.

"So we go into the studio in Costa Mesa, and I'm in there with this guy. Now, there are a lot of producers who do what's called 'comping'. It basically means that I go out there, listen to the track, just play some guitar licks, then we'll listen back to them at the end and there might be one really cool lick that we stick in there. This guy had me do about eleven guitar tracks on almost every song – and he basically put it all on there. So if you listen to that Transition album, the way the guitars are done makes Def Leppard sound like Muddy Waters. It was turned into a pop album.

"It was too bad, because there were songs on there I'm really proud of to this day. One is Running In Place. There's a ballad called Face The Night, about one time that Marie and I had a huge battle and she had left. Got To Kill The Monkey came about when Marie said, 'Why don't you write a tune about air pollution?' Transition was the name of the Philly clinic where I worked as a drug counselor, and I wrote the title track thinking about the people I met.

"If those songs had been recorded the way I do it now with Eric Corne, they could have been really cool. They were just overdone. It sounded like a Phil

Spector record, and I love Phil Spector, but that's not what I do. Also, the more I tried to write bluesy stuff, the more I was told, 'No, you've gotta have hits and hooks'. I'd come out in the UK and Scandinavia as a raw blues-rock guitarist, but these guys tried to turn me into some kind of insipid pop act. It was like they'd taken away the essence of what I am."

I went through a phase when we toured with a juicer. On our rider, we had all these raw vegetables and I was downing huge glasses of carrot juice. People would come into our dressing room expecting hookers and cocaine, and find vegetables and Perrier. The road was a different thing.

On the road, at least, no puppet-master could tamper with Walter's vision. He remembers the early-1990s as a time of near-masochistic touring, and the diary a hectic scrawl of tarmac-scorching engagements, survivable only due to his new lifestyle. By this point, freebase had been replaced by five-a-day: "I went through a phase when we toured

with a juicer. On our rider, we had all these raw vegetables and I was downing huge glasses of carrot juice. People would come into our dressing room expecting hookers and cocaine, and find vegetables and Perrier. The road was a different thing."

It was all relative. What Walter deemed a quiet life would still constitute force-ten mayhem for any other band. "Back then, we had a keyboard player called Mongo," he remembers. "He was a great musician and I loved him, but he had a problem with drugs and was trying to keep it hidden from us. One time, we were on a ferry and about to get off in Sweden, so we asked Mongo, 'Do you have any drugs on you?' Because at that point, they were very intense in Sweden. It was, like, life in jail for drugs.

"Anyway, Mongo told us he didn't have anything. So we got off the ferry and the border guards made our van pull over into this area with a fence around it. That's when Mongo goes, 'I just remembered, I got a bunch of hash and weed on me'. Oh fuck, right? So Mongo hands this stuff to Jimmy, and asks him to do something with it. To which Jimmy, who didn't even smoke pot, goes, 'Fuck you, Mongo'. They made us all get out of the van. They took us all into separate rooms and did the rubber-glove test, up the ass.

"After that, Mongo managed to stuff the weed into a little trash can we had in the van. They were waiting to get a dope-sniffing dog, and there were some guys who were in training to be border guards. Mongo took the trash can from the van, smiled at these trainees and said, 'Hey, you guys mind if I just put this in the dumpster?' 'No, go ahead'. So he dumped the shit in the dumpster and they never found it. After we got out of that one, we sat in a circle with Mongo in the middle, and took turns going off on him."

Opposite: Walter: "I drank so much carrot juice in the early-'90s that when we went to Denmark, the promoter pulled Marie aside and told her he was very worried about me because I'd turned orange. He thought I was ill, when I was actually at the peak of health I'd been at for years. I am a little orange in that picture."

The band weren't the only ones butting heads. In 1992, Walter found himself drawn into a third round with an off-and-on adversary. "Albert King is one guy I never got along with," he says of the late blues legend. "There had already been a couple of incidents.

"Back in Canned Heat, we opened for Albert King in San Francisco. Being the support act, our dressing room didn't have a bathroom; we were supposed to use the public one, all the way at the front door of this huge club. We were ready to go on, but man, I needed to piss. A show is ninety minutes, right, so if you don't piss, you got a problem.

"So I knock on the door of Albert King's dressing room and he's sitting there, all by himself. He's got on his Flying V and he's tuning up. I said, 'Hey man, I'm Walter and I play with Canned Heat. I was just wondering if I could take a piss in your bathroom?' Albert says, 'No, this toilet's for the headliner'. I say, 'Yeah, but y'know, we're ready to go on, and we don't have a bathroom. I just need to run in there and piss, man'. He tells me, 'No, get the fuck out of here'. So the bouncers had to escort me through the crowd of 2000 people to the public bathroom. It probably held the show up for fifteen minutes."

Round two: "Another time, we were doing a gig in Philly with Mayall. It was a big outdoor show and Coco was playing a solo, when all of a sudden, Albert King runs out on the stage. He wasn't even on the bill, but he gets in front of Coco and starts yelling, 'I hear you're stealing my shit on guitar!' Poor Coco, who worshipped the guy, was looking around like, 'What the fuck?'

"So now, years later, we're opening for Albert King at the Birmingham Town Hall with my solo band. My keyboard player at the time used a Roland Jazz Chorus, which is the amp Albert King used for his guitar. So we played our set,

our roadies packed up the gear, we stood in the back and Albert is ready to go on. Jimmy says to him, 'It's a great band you have, Mr King'. Very respectful. And Albert King says to him: 'Who the fuck are you?' Jimmy just said, 'Well, I'm nobody. Don't worry about it'.

"Well, Albert goes on, and as we're watching, his amp starts to fuck up. He's kicking the amp, he's cussing, and his amp finally stops working. So his road manager comes running up and says, 'Hey, you guys got a Roland Jazz Chorus,

Albert King should have let me take a piss eight years ago. Then I'd have gladly handed him the amp. But I'm sorry, dude – that piss cost him £150.

right?' And I say, 'Yeah, but it's gonna cost him £150'. This road manager says, 'Are you fucking kidding me? That's Albert King! He needs an amp!' I said, 'Look, it's not for me. It's gonna require my roadies to go to the trailer and bring the amp in, so I want you to give them each £75. And actually, I don't give a fuck if Albert King uses this amp or not'. It wasn't revenge. It was just give-and-take. If you're kind to me, I'll give it back,

and I'm not a vindictive guy. I'd pretty much do anything for anybody, as long as it's sort of reciprocated and I'm not treated like dog-shit on someone's shoes.

"So this tour manager pulls the money out, goes up to my roadies and throws the money at them, all disgusted. They bring in the amp. Albert does the gig. And at the end of the night, the road manager comes up and says, 'I can't fucking believe you charged Albert King to use your guitar amp. Who the fuck do you think you are?' And I said, 'Well, you know what? Albert King should have let me take a piss eight years ago. Then I'd have gladly handed him the amp. But I'm sorry, dude – that piss cost him £150.'"

Playing live, 1991

SAY WHAT YOU MEAN

Perspiration had paid off. By 1993, Walter's solo flag was planted deep in foreign fields. Scandinavia swooned. Holland sat up and begged. The blues strongholds of mainland Europe fell like dominos. Frustrating, then, that to fly home was to feel his powers diminish. In the United States, Walter could draw a crowd anywhere you stuck a pin, but tumbleweed blew through record stores when you requested his solo records.

"I had a good deal with Provogue, which meant they financed the records and owned them for Europe," he says. "I owned them for the rest of the world, so I was free to go out and shop them in America, try and get them released. I took all those early solo records around the States and nobody was interested. I could go to record labels and tell them I'd had a hit record that outsold Bon Jovi, and they'd be like, 'We don't give a shit. Leave us alone'.

"I called every agency, including guys from the Mayall years, saying that I wanted to get going in the States. They'd just say, 'We're not interested. You're not going anywhere. Nothing's gonna happen for you'. It was like, 'Wait a minute, I've sold almost a million records in Europe. I've headlined Parkpop and the Shepherd's Bush Empire'. Like, what the hell?"

Then a flash of possibility: "I was given a chance to get onto Silvertone in Holland, which was the label that Mayall and Buddy Guy were on. They told me that if I signed, they'd distribute my album in America. So I went to the

owner of Provogue, who had been good to me, and said, 'Look man, I got a chance to get a record out in the States. You can't do that for me and I can't do it on my own. Is there a way you would let me out of our contract?' And he was very fair. He said, 'Look, I don't want to hold you back…'"

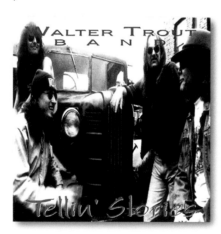

So began Walter's deal with Silvertone, and an album – 1994's Tellin' Stories – that haunts him to this day. "It was a nightmare with these guys. First, they told me there was this female singer, who

I will not name here, and that I had to have her on my record and call it 'Walter Trout Presents…'. It was like, who the fuck am I, Elton John? Nobody in this country knows who I am and you want me to 'present' this girl? I remember getting into a violent argument in a restaurant and saying, 'No, it's a deal-breaker, I'm not gonna sign with you'. After I said I refused to have this girl, they said, 'OK'.

"Then I said I wanted to record the album in LA, because the whole band lived there. They said, 'No, you've got to do the album in London'. So they gave me a huge budget, but made me pay out of that to use their studio in London, which was, like, two grand a day. They made me use their house producer and pay him out of the budget. They owned a house in London and they put Marie and I up in there, with another house for the band – both of which we paid rent on. So they gave me this huge budget, but I paid it right back to them, immediately."

Opposite: Promo shot for Silvertone Records, 1993

WALTER TROUT

Promotional shot for Silvertone. London, 1993

Tellin' Stories was another case of good songs suffocated by the pillow of bad production. "There were great moments," remembers Walter. "Bernie Marsden came in and we wrote and sang together on Somebody's Cryin'. Micky Moody played a slide solo on Head Hung Down. But the sound they were getting in the studio was horrendous. It was dog-shit. They would mix and there was no bottom end. It didn't even sound like I had a bass player.

"The producer, who shall remain nameless, had a great résumé, and had been the engineer on Buddy Guy's Damn Right I've Got The Blues. He literally said to me, 'We don't add the bass when we mix. When we master the record, *then* we add the bass'. Now, this is when I knew I was getting fucked over, and that Silvertone wanted this record to sound like shit. Because the mixes should have the sound as good as it can get. Then, with mastering, you just adjust the levels.

"So they put Tellin' Stories out, and it sounded horrific. The band sounds tiny, and it's difficult to even hear there's a bass player. My manager at the time – this is before Marie took over – went to the offices of Silvertone in New York, and they wouldn't even speak to him about it. He had seen the head of Silvertone at a trade show, and he'd gone up and said, 'Hey, I just want to discuss my client, Walter Trout, who's on your label'. The guy had said, 'We don't want to know about Walter Trout, just fuck off'. So I was a tax write-off for them. Because I wouldn't put that chick on the record, they said, 'Fuck you'.

"At which point, I realised I had made a massive mistake, because whatever leverage and name I had in Europe – and this was my fourth album – they were destroying it because they weren't pushing the record. So in Europe, where I did have a career, they were sabotaging it… and there was still nothing happening in the States!"

Tail between legs, Walter began the mea culpas: "So I called up the head of Provogue to say very humbly that I'd made a huge mistake, that I was really sorry, I'd given up trying to have a career in America – and was there any way I could

get back on the label, because at least I was appreciated with them. He said to me, 'Yes, I'll take you back, but Silvertone are not going to let you go. Even if they are using you for a tax write-off, if they have you for a three or four-album deal, you're screwed, and you can't get out of it'.

"So I sat around for a while and formulated a plan. Back in the day, to stay out of Vietnam, I'd gone to Camden County Community College, where I had

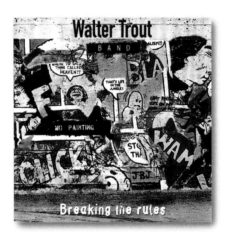

As I wept uncontrollably, I told him I was through with the music business, it was making me a mental wreck, I needed psychological help, I didn't want to see a guitar again and I was having a mental breakdown. I told him I couldn't stand the thought of even hearing music and I just wanted to get the fuck out of this contract. Just weeping and freaking out.

studied acting. I thought to myself, this is the only shot I have to get out of it. I couldn't use lawyers. So I whipped into my best Stanislavski. I called up Silvertone, got through to a secretary and

told her I needed to speak to the head of the label. She didn't want to put me through, so I started crying and pretending to have a nervous breakdown. Finally, she says, 'Hold on', and puts me through.

"As I wept uncontrollably, I told him I was through with the music business, it was making me a mental wreck, I needed psychological help, I didn't want to see a guitar again and I was having a mental breakdown. I told him I couldn't stand the thought of even hearing music and I just wanted to get the fuck out of this contract. Just weeping and freaking out. Finally, he said, 'OK, we'll let you go'. Still crying, I said, 'Please, would you send me a registered letter with your signature saying the contract is null and void?' He agreed. I said, 'Thank you so much. I'm so glad to be out of this fucked-up business. I'm gonna go get psychiatric help and figure out what I want to do with my life, but it's certainly gonna have nothing to do with music'.

"Then I hung up the phone and started laughing uncontrollably. I was out of the deal. It really was an Oscar-winning performance. He sent me the letter. I faxed the letter over to Provogue, and a week later I was back with them. A month later, I was in the studio making my next record. Like, 'I'm done crying now. Music ain't so bad. I think I *will* play the guitar after all'."

Appropriately, the next track from Walter was To Begin Again, leading the charge for 1995's restorative Breaking The Rules, which was the first album deal negotiated by Marie. "I chose to call it that," he explains, "because as far as being a bluesman, I was always breaking the rules. With the artwork, Marie and I were walking down by the beach at Huntington. There was this big wall down there, and the town had put up one of those little black stencil signs that said 'No Painting'. These graffiti artists had come down in the night and painted all this incredible stuff – but left the black stencil sign with 'No Painting'. I saw that and I said to Marie, 'Now *that's* breaking the rules'. That wall ended up being the album cover.'"

Live at the Skanderborg Festival, 1995

Above: Audience interaction at the Skanderborg Festival, 1995

As well as breaking the rules as a bluesman, Walter was also shattering his stereotype as a hellraiser. On June 6th 1993, the guitarist and Marie had welcomed their first son, Jonathan Cooper Brændgaard Trout, and now, on March 11th, 1996, the family became a four-piece with the arrival of Michael Edward Brændgaard Trout. "Becoming a father was terrifying," remembers Walter. "But I was really ready and dove in. I wanted to be a hands-on father. I remember my older brother telling me that he couldn't have kids because he could never change diapers. Well, I loved changing diapers, actually. I would play games with the baby, tickle him, and sing to him. I thought it was great fun. Marie and the kids spent every summer touring with us, and I have to say, those were the greatest days of my life. At that point, the road changed from debauchery to actually meaning something. And I changed too."

Next, in 1997, came the game-changing album. "Positively Beale Street was great," remembers Walter. "Coco had called me up one day and told me he'd just made a record with this great producer down in Memphis called Jim Gaines. He said this guy had heard my stuff and thought I was great, and that I should give him a call. So I called Jim up, and he was just the nicest guy in the world; a true Southern gentleman. And he says, 'I'd love to work with you'.

"So for the next record, we went into the Beale Street Studios with Jim. It had been a well-known studio for a long time, and Jim had produced tons of bands there, including a lot of the stuff he did for Luther Allison. It was an old nightclub and it still looked like one: it was very long and narrow, with a stage at one end. Right after we finished the album, the place got sold to the Hard Rock Cafe, so my record was the last one recorded there. They had a wall leading into the control room that had been signed by everyone: Al Green, Booker T Jones, 'Duck' Dunn, Steve Cropper, Eddie Floyd, Otis Redding. It's still there in the Hard Rock, but now it's in the kitchen.

"Recording that album was a great

experience. I don't have a favourite album, but I do have favourite songs, and one that had a lot of meaning at the time was Song For A Wanderer. Some people can't stomach it, because I sing in falsetto, but I wrote it for my brother, who always loved R&B groups like the Delfonics and Stylistics.

"At the end of those sessions, I just needed a title. I had this revelation that all of the really indigenous American musical forms had originated right there

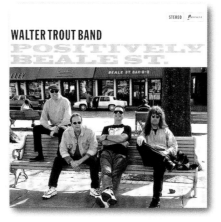

in the Mississippi Delta. Rockabilly, country, rock 'n' roll, R&B, blues, gospel, all of it. So I decided to make that album title my homage to Beale Street, and also to the Bob Dylan song, Positively 4th Street."

This was a classic American record, bottled in an iconic Southern studio, tipping its hat to the nation's musical heritage – so it was apt that Positively Beale Street would become Walter's first Stateside release (where it was retitled as simply Walter Trout). "When it was done," he recalls, "I said to myself, 'Now here's another record that nobody in the States is gonna be interested in'. Then Jim hooked me up with Thomas Ruf at Ruf Records, and lo and behold he and his stateside business partner, Ira Leslie, were suddenly pushing me in the United States. I ended up making a few records in Memphis with Jim, like Livin' Every Day, in 1999, which I think is another really good album."

Not everything Walter touched down in Memphis turned to gold. On May 6th, 2000, the Tennessee city was also the

backdrop to one of his most memorable gaffes. "We were playing at the Beale Street Music Festival," he remembers, "and it was the same night that Dickey Betts got fired from the Allman Brothers. We were there in the wings listening, and we were all going, 'It sounds like Dickey Betts is playing in the wrong key – what's he doing?' The next day, it was announced via fax that he had been fired from his own band.

"Ike Turner was also there, and he was walking around with the most beautiful woman I've ever seen in my life. Drop-dead, lose-your-breath beautiful, y'know? So I go into our dressing room, which was this RV, and there's that mischievous son-of-a-bitch best friend of mine, Jimmy Trapp, sitting there. I say, 'Did you see the woman with Ike Turner? She's unbelievable. What the fuck is she doing with Ike Turner? Didn't she see the movie?'

"Jimmy just looks at me and smiles, and I start going off, loudly saying things like, 'I guess she must love having the shit beat out of her'. I'm going and going, and Jimmy is just sitting there with this grin on his face, not saying a word. All of a sudden, right in the middle of this, as I'm screaming and going off, the little bathroom door opens in our RV – and out walks Ike Turner.

"He had to go to the bathroom and Jimmy, being no Albert King, had let Ike use our RV. He walked out and I just went 'Erm…'. Jimmy was just laughing, hand over his mouth. And I'm looking at Jimmy like, 'You son of a bitch. Fuck you, Trapp!'

"Ike walked up to me, and I'm just speechless. I'm ready to get hit, like, this guy is gonna deck me. But he just said, 'Hi, I'm Ike'. And I said, 'Er, I'm Walter'. He never mentioned it, but he'd heard the whole thing. And when he left, Jimmy's like, 'Hey, you're the one that went off, Trout. I was just sat here listening'. So I'm known as the king of the faux pas down there in Memphis."

Opposite: Recording Positively Beale Street at Beale Street Studios, Memphis with producer, Jim Gaines

HELPIN' HAND

Just for a heartbeat, the post-millennium twinkled with possibility and rained personal triumphs. On August 9th, 2001, Walter and Marie added a third son, Dylan Scott Brændgaard Trout, to their burgeoning family and tourbus. That same summer, the bandleader was enjoying lunch with Bob Harris when the influential British broadcaster slid across his autobiography, The Whispering Years, in which Walter was named as the world's greatest rock guitarist. "I thanked Bob profusely. It was hard for me to believe. But he said, 'I called you that because you invest more in your playing than anybody else.'"

In the music industry, long-bolted doors hung open, with Detroit duo The White Stripes dragging the blues into hipster magazines and onto radio playlists with 2001's White Blood Cells. Walter welcomed the sentiment, if not always the songs: "Jack White is someone I respect greatly, but it's not like I can't wait to get home and put his records on. His playing, I always found, didn't have a lot of finesse. I was raised with guys like Bloomfield, B.B. King, Clapton, Hendrix. Those guys had a touch. It wasn't all wild and crazy."

And then, on September 11th, American Airlines Flight 11 and United Airlines Flight 175 loomed over the New York skyline, and this gleaming new dawn was streaked with blood. "Go The Distance had been out a little while when 9/11 happened," says Walter. "The title song became somewhat of an anthem over here. I was supposed to be playing a gig in Dayton, Ohio, that night. I called the club owner and said, 'We're cancelling, right?' But he told me, 'No, I'm getting calls from people and they want this gig to happen'.

"We almost couldn't get to the venue, because the country was in turmoil. Everybody was buying up gasoline because they thought there wasn't going to be any more from the Middle East. When we finally got there, I started singing that song, and instead of the line

'I'm gonna go the distance', I sang, 'We're gonna go the distance'. The whole place just started sobbing, and I was crying too, up there at the mic. We had a couple of minutes of silence, and I gave a little speech about what it meant to live in America.

"I sorta became their therapy leader that night. And about three or four days after that show, we rented a studio in St. Louis and re-recorded Go The Distance, but made that line plural and sang 'We'. We started selling that at gigs and donated all the money to the victims' fund. To this day, when I go back to Dayton, they ask me to play that song, but sing 'We' instead of 'I.'"

One of the most poignant nights of Walter's career, that snap decision to

switch lyrics in Ohio was also a reminder that the guitarist was often at his impulsive best on the stage. Two years later, Relentless hammered the point home. There had been live solo releases before, from 1992's No More Fish Jokes to 2000's Face The Music, but the two shows recorded May 2003 in Amsterdam were different. Rather than sleepwalk through a setlist of old chestnuts, this was a rock 'n' roll high-wire act, with brand-new material birthed in front of a live crowd – and no safety net.

For the concept, all credit to Marie: "I was lying in bed one night and woke up with this eureka moment. I couldn't think of any band that would be able to record new material live. But I knew Walter's band could do it, because these guys are unbelievable. I thought we should have a DVD, too, because then people could see the fingers moving and know it wasn't just a bunch of overdubs after the fact. Walter thought the idea was a little crazy at first…"

"In hindsight," picks up Walter, "there had been a couple of albums done like that, but they hadn't been marketed that way. Running On Empty by Jackson Browne was an album of new songs played live, but you had no idea until the first song ended and the applause came in. Neil Young had done one, too. But they hadn't made it their selling-point.

"Marie and I looked at a few clubs in LA, but they just didn't feel right. At that point, Thomas Ruf asked me, 'Where's your favourite club to play?' I told him it was the Paradiso, and he said, 'Well, let's do it there'. There were all these film trucks from Dutch national television. Jim Gaines had come over from Memphis, and Ira Leslie flew in from New York. Ruf had brought in an entire film crew from the Ohne Filter music programme, and they'd hung mics through the whole place to have the sound in 5.1 surround for the DVD. So it was high pressure.

"If you're doing a gig and you flub a lyric, nobody gives a shit. But when it's being recorded, you can't go back. So I'm trying to look like I'm having a great time up there, but because these were brand-new originals, I'm having to look down at the lyric-sheets on the floor by the monitors.

"We recorded two nights, and if we hadn't got it right, we'd have been screwed. In the end, we used pretty much all of the second night. And on the DVD, we kept the bit where Ira comes out to introduce us wearing an angel outfit, so stoned that he couldn't even pronounce Paradiso. It's all on there. We wouldn't take it off the DVD, so he was pissed about that."

As an album title, Relentless neatly encapsulated Walter's bulldozer attitude to fashion and fad. In the post-millennium, the word might equally have applied to Jimmy Trapp, whose carousing was watched by the band through their fingers. "Some of the shit I could tell you about that guy," says Walter. "If I saw someone like this in a movie, I wouldn't believe it. I'd never met a person so out of his mind, in a good way. He was pure entertainment.

"He had six or seven alter-egos that could kick in at any time. One of them, for instance, was Disco Dick. We'd go into a bar or a disco, and he'd have to get drunk first, and then he would take on this persona. He'd do a perfect Russian accent, go up to the DJ, get right up in his face and say, 'I am Disco Dick, ze famous Russian disco star! Zis music zat you play – zis iz not disco! True disco music iz 110 beats per minute! Boom-cha! Boom-cha! Boom-cha!'

"Here's a typical Jimmy story. In 2003, we were at the Hoffbräuhaus in Munich: the place where Hitler started his group. Jimmy was Jewish, and he was sitting there getting more and more pissed off. There were all these girls from Canada with us, and Jimmy is going, 'Girls, I don't know if you realise this, but I'm a very well-known Broadway and opera singer, and I do a great version of The Sound Of Music'. So the rest of the band all played up to this and we're like, 'Yeah, just wait until you hear this guy, you won't believe it'.

"The girls are going, 'Oh please, we want to hear you sing', but Jimmy says he needs more beers first. He's getting drunker and drunker, until finally he's ready. The balcony in the Hoffbräuhaus where Hitler used to speak from is closed now, but it's still there. So Jimmy gets up,

rips the tablecloth off the table, wraps it around his head. He moves the barrier and he walks right up on Hitler's fricking balcony and stands there looking over the place, with 600 people all waiting to see what he does.

"We've spent all day telling these girls what a great opera singer Jimmy is, and he suddenly screams, in the most horrific screeching voice with no discernible melody: 'The hiiiiills are aliiiiive!' He just belts it out, y'know? The whole place stops. Then he whips off the tablecloth and 600 drunk patrons rose to their feet and gave him a rousing standing ovation. You'd see that in a movie and think, 'Nobody would do that shit in public'. Well, Jimmy Trapp did."

With Jimmy around, the laughter never stopped, but in these latter years, it was laced with the sense the bassist was reaching terminal velocity. "It was just constant with Jimmy," remembers Walter. "He was always either drunk or hungover. He'd say to us, 'Fuck, I've got the flu again today'. In 2005, he had a

I have a long list of great friends who are now dead, because they didn't take the hint they needed to change their habits. Jimmy Trapp was one of the greatest people I ever knew. There has never, in my whole life, been a character like that guy. I was best man at his wedding. He was best man at mine. He was my best friend, for sure.

quintuple bypass, five veins in his heart replaced, and one week after that, he was down at the bar, rip-roaring drunk.

"Now, I had hernia surgery in 2013 and it took me a month to even get up and walk around. With his operation, his whole chest had been ripped open: it's major surgery. And one week after that, he was getting fucked-up again. He only lasted three months after that. He just couldn't quit. He died on August 24th, 2005.

"I have a long list of great friends who are now dead, because they didn't take the hint they needed to change their habits. Jimmy Trapp was one of the greatest people I ever knew. There has never, in my whole life, been a character like that guy. I was best man at his wedding. He was best man at mine. He was my best friend, for sure."

Opposite: Walter does the Best Man duties at Jimmy's wedding in 1988
Above: Jimmy backstage in Denmark, 1989

Nothing to do but play on. Even as dear friends left the building, new ones arrived, with Rick Knapp bolstering the Trout band on bass, and Walter revelling in his avuncular role to a generation of young bluesmen including Oli Brown, Laurence Jones and Mitch Laddie. Whether through his words of guidance, guitar lessons, shop-window support slots or effusive soundbites on tour flyers, Walter gave many artists their break, and behind the scenes, his battered Strat was working overtime. In 1999, the guitarist had guested on the eponymous debut of British gunslinger Aynsley Lister, and now, in 2005, he wept lead lines over the title track of Danny Bryant's Days Like This.

"Walter has always been there supporting me," says Danny, "and I honestly don't think I'd have this job or lifestyle if it wasn't for him. When I was about 14, my parents bought the Prisoner Of A Dream album on vinyl. Then we were out shopping in Cambridge and there was a poster up for Walter's gig at The Junction, so I asked if we could go. It changed my life.

"The album Walter had out then was Breaking The Rules," continues Danny, "so I just sent him a fan letter, and put in a picture of me holding my guitar. When he got back from that tour, he rang up, and we chatted for an hour. Whenever he came to the UK, I'd go to his hotel, we'd sit outside with two guitars and he'd give me guitar lessons. We've become proper friends."

Walter has good reasons for supporting the cubs: "It all goes back to that meeting with Duke Ellington. I came out so moved and wanting to be just like that man. Then, five years later, I met Buddy

Rich, and he made me think that if all musicians were like that, then I didn't want to be one. I'd gone into a music store in Philadelphia. Buddy Rich was in there with another guy, standing at the counter, buying drumsticks. I walked up and said, 'Excuse me, Mr Rich. Is there any chance I could get your autograph for my dad? He's your biggest fan'. As respectful and humble as I could be.

"Buddy Rich just turned around and went at me. I remember him going, 'You little asshole! Who the fuck do you think you are?' He started yelling, and his voice got louder and louder, then he physically grabbed me and attacked me. I remember being on the ground. I don't remember if I fell to get away from him, or if he pushed me down, but the guy who was with him pulled him off. Buddy got up and he was like, 'You fucking little prick!'

"It was pretty traumatic. After that, I went to my dad, and I said, 'Hey Dad, I met Buddy Rich today, and I'd like you to do me a favour. Please don't ever play his music or mention his name again when I'm in the house'.

"To this day, I've had eleven drummers come through my band, and they all want to play Buddy Rich, but it's not permitted. If you want to listen to him, you put on fucking headphones. I don't care if he's the second coming of the Messiah. I don't care if no other drummer on the face of the earth is worthy to carry his fucking underpants. I don't give a shit. I'm not hearing him in my band."

From that day forward, Walter resolved to give newcomers the support he had received from Ellington, rather than the abuse he suffered at the hands of Rich. Often, he remembers, they paid him back with inspiration or a fresh perspective.

This spread: Supporting the Cubs. Walter shares some banter and a smile with British blues guitarist and singer-songwriter, Danny Bryant **Above:** Walter and a 15-year-old Danny in 1995

"The seed of the Full Circle album in 2006 was planted by recording with Danny. I thought it'd be great to have guys just come in and jam, and then after we'd written a song together, we'd record it live. It was an experiment, and the label and Marie all thought I was nuts.

"I went in the studio without any ideas. It was all very spontaneous. The first day, John Mayall came in at eleven in the morning. I suggested a slow blues in C minor, and asked him to play acoustic piano, because a lot of people haven't heard just how beautiful he plays it. That first song we did – She Takes More Than She Gives – is one of the best things I've ever recorded, because John's piano is just so sympathetic to what I'm doing on guitar. Then we did Highway Song, which was like the Stones meets Chuck Berry.

"When John left, two hours later, we already had two songs done. Then Joe Bonamassa came into the studio, and after about an hour we had Clouds On The Horizon. He left, I had dinner, then Guitar Shorty came in and we did Wrapped Around Your Finger. So I had three guys come through the studio in one day and we got four tracks. Sometimes, it's good to keep it simple. Just three chords and a jam, instead of trying to write Sgt Pepper."

Even now, deep into his fifties, the songs kept coming, with each new album acting as a momentary release-valve for

Walter's creative backlog. By 2008, the guitarist was ready to deliver another bar-raising album, with The Outsider guided by John Porter's production from the open-tuned strum of Turn Your Eyes To Heaven to the Stones-flavoured groove of The Restless Age. Best of all was the climactic title track, whose lyric scotched any notion that Walter was now a feet-under-table member of the blues establishment.

"That song started off being about someone I know and ended up being about me," he explains. "I realised after I wrote it that in parts of the blues community, I'm still an outsider. They don't know what to do with me, but I just keep going. You don't become an artist to mould your creations around what you think people want you to be.

"At that point, you're just a prostitute. Everybody divides opinion. My mother loved Elvis: my father couldn't stand him. I'm a Beatles freak and I have a good friend who will leave the room if I play a Beatles record. So it's not just me."

As a musician, Walter had long recognised the futility of striving for universal appeal, but on 2010's Common Ground, he returned with a set of songs that called for compromise in the bearpit of modern politics. "That album was really a call for people to be more forgiving to each other," he explains. "Those songs were written during election time here in the United States, amidst all the yelling and screaming from the left and the right.

"It just felt like there was this inability amongst our politicians to be civilised and meet in the middle. Nobody was trying to come up with ways of actually making life better for people, they were just screaming that you were a fucking idiot if you were voting for Obama or McCain.

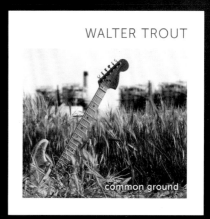

"And meanwhile, there's no funding for schools, they're cutting food stamps, the roads are horrific and the bridges are literally falling down when you're trying to drive across middle America. I'm not one of those guys that loves the 'good old days'. I actually think a lot of things about the good old days sucked. I think people look at shit through rose-coloured glasses. But I do see that the world is changing, and I'm not sure it's all for the good. That's where Blues For The Modern Daze came from. And I don't know if I'll ever match the statement I made with that record…"

This spread: Walter backstage

BLUES FOR THE MODERN DAZE

The best songwriting advice Walter Trout ever received came during pillow-talk. "This was back when I was first starting to write songs," he remembers. "I was with this wild and crazy Italian girl, Denise 'Muffin' Muffucci, who loved blues. This girl told me there were two blues themes that you have to stay away from. She says, 'Theme number one is that my baby left me and I'm bummed out'. And it's true: there are a lot of those. Then she says, 'Theme number two is, 'I'll buy you a Cadillac if you'll sit on my face'. So I always tried to stay clear of those."

The relationship sank, but the advice stuck. While lesser writers flicked the autopilot, Walter had bled onto his lyric-sheets since the days of Wilmont Mews, mining everything from his troubled youth to the disturbing trend of school-shooters in modern America. Now, as he readied a new studio album in early 2012, the songwriter surveyed a world that demanded commentary.

Since 2007, the global recession had cut deep, killing jobs, hiking debt, razing entire industries and communities. The twin conflicts instigated in Afghanistan and Iraq during the presidency of George W. Bush remained rivers of blood.

In the States, a gulf between rich and poor had been opened up with a crowbar, with Wall Street leaders clinking glasses as Main Street punters queued for soup. With Barack Obama's first term widely deemed a damp squib, the GOP's candidate, Mitt Romney, hovered in the wings with his nefarious manifesto. On television: The X Factor and American Idol.

Hard times – but the human race was no pushover. If the spirit of revolution was palpable in the Occupy movement and the Arab Spring, then Blues For The

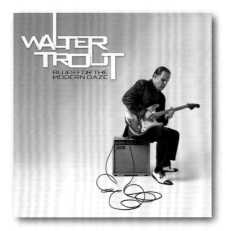

Modern Daze provided the ultimate soundtrack. "That was my most political album by far," remembers Walter. "I'm very affected by what I see in the world and I felt like I had something to say. I think you can gauge from those songs that the insidious corporate takeover of the democratic system in the States is really frightening to me. And how many wars are we gonna have? I really had some stuff to get off my chest there."

In an age of toothless production-line pop, the songs co-produced by Walter and Eric Corne at Entourage Studios – alongside the hard-working Trout road band of Sammy Avila, Rick Knapp and

Michael Leasure – were polemics. The Sky Is Fallin' Down fused gallows humour to a stinging country-blues lick. Money Rules The World took potshots at the fat cats lining the corporate trough, while Lifestyle Of The Rich And Famous charted the fall of a bankrupt magnate.

Brother's Keeper riffed on the intolerance of the US hardcore Christian right, while album-closer Pray For Rain sounded timeless, played on a thrift-store acoustic, mixed in mono, and taking the perspective of a farmer ruined by drought. "I wrote that whole album in two weeks," remembers Walter, "but it felt like it wasn't even me writing it. It came from somewhere else."

Modern Daze wasn't pure politics. Featuring organ by Deacon Jones, Turn Off Your TV took a wry swipe at the brain-drain experience of channel-hopping. "With that one, I wasn't really feeling anger," explains Walter. "I had just been watching TV at home in America. I have a thousand channels, so when I get home from a gig, it takes a good hour to get through them all, and by the time you do, you realise there's nothing there. Then you see all the shit they're trying to sell you and it gets rather disgusting."

This spread: Shots from the photo session for the Blues For The Modern Daze album

Lonely, meanwhile, had been scrawled onto a Starbucks napkin as Walter watched mute strangers tap at laptops and smartphones. "It doesn't seem like the whole tech explosion is increasing our understanding of each other at all," he says. "In some ways, it's increasing the polarisation, and driving people further apart into little tribal groups. It seems like there's always some electronic gadget that we need between us to communicate.

"I've had people tell me I'm just a bitter old man and I don't get it. Well, OK. But I was around before the Internet, of course, and I remember when conversation was an art, and we didn't sit across from each other at the table texting. I feel like attention spans are getting shorter and shorter. People don't want to read a novel. They want a headline, and it'd better not go over 140 characters, or it's too much for their attention spans to take in.

"Alongside that," he continues, "since the computer age, a lot of people have this idea that music should be free to the masses. That's bullshit. Artists spend their youth locked up in their rooms, learning an instrument, putting thousands upon thousands of hours into becoming a player. They deserve to be rewarded for their efforts, just like in any other line of work."

Elsewhere, Modern Daze's more personal moments suggested that Walter's headspace remained a warzone to rival the outside world, with Saw My Mama Cryin' frankly recalling occasions when Lynnette's stoical mask slipped, and Recovery admitting the guitarist still felt the rank breath of addiction on his neck. "Anyone who has come out the other side of that experience," he says, "is aware of their proclivity to go in that direction.

"I can't imagine being fucked-up now, but I remember one time in England when I came close to a wobble. This was in Colne, around 1991. First off, I was getting my guitar out of the van when

We must have taken a hundred photos where I'm in the military shirts. We took just a couple with the jacket – and that's what they picked. The morning we were leaving for the shoot, I had the horrible realisation that I had thrown out my dress shoes. So I ran into the garage and found these blue-and-white shoes that cost me $19... and they ended up on the cover!

the roadie we had at the time drove off. I jumped out of the way and came within about three inches of being run over and killed. So I was freaked out. Then Marie and I had one of our gigantic battles: one of the biggest in our twenty-four years.

"I said 'Fuck this' and went down to the hotel bar. I told my manager at the time that I'd had it and I was gonna get fucked-up, and he asked the barman to get me a double-shot of Jack. That was put in front of me, when all of a sudden, Jimmy appeared, grabbed me by the collar and told me, 'Trout, if you touch that glass, I'm gonna beat the living shit

out of you. If you even attempt to drink it, I'm gonna pound your fucking face'. Now that's a true friend. So Jimmy saved the day – and that manager was a fucking idiot."

It's hard to guess what Jimmy would have made of the Modern Daze sleeve, on which Walter ditched his familiar waistcoats to cut a dash in suit jacket and two-tone brogues. "I had gone out and bought some really cool army shirts with epaulettes and stuff," he recalls. "I was thinking that I had some Occupy Wall Street music on this album and I'm gonna go military. Y'know, like we're gonna kick some ass. But Marie said, 'Well, I'm gonna bring the suit you wore to the Blues Awards in Memphis to the shoot'.

"We must have taken a hundred photos where I'm in the military shirts. We took just a couple with the jacket – and that's what they picked. The morning we were leaving for the shoot, I had the horrible realisation that I had thrown out my dress shoes. So I ran into the garage and found these blue-and-white shoes that cost me $19... and they ended up on the cover!"

Released in April 2012, Modern Daze came out fighting, scoring starburst reviews, topping polls, shifting units and establishing that far from being a relic of blues-gone-by, Walter was amongst the sharpest chroniclers of the new era. "That album advanced my career," he says. "I got reviews saying I'd become the populist voice of blues, comparing me to the modern electric-blues version of Woody Guthrie. That felt good. I was driving around a while back, listening to Modern Daze, and it kinda blew my mind. It was like, 'Wow, did I write that?' I almost feel like it's gonna be hard to beat that one."

The accolades kept coming. Patently, he was going to need a bigger mantelpiece. And yet, given the eloquent, satirical, heart-on-sleeve dazzle of his Modern Daze songwriting, Walter was darkly amused to learn that Blues For My Baby – the one song that arguably skirted cliché, written while the guitarist pined for an out-of-town Marie – had scored a major industry award. "I had decided I would write about that 'my baby left me' theme just once," he remembers, "and then iTunes chose it as the Best Blues Song of 2012."

Walter had rarely been more visible. "That October," he remembers, "I was invited to play at the premiere of B.B. King's Life Of Riley in London, by the director Jon Brewer. Jon invited Mick Taylor to jam with me and we just had a great time. Jeff Beck was there and I invited him up to play, told him, 'I got a

spare Strat and it would just be a dream if you would get up and jam'. But he told us he'd been drinking for three days and didn't feel like playing!"

In early 2013, as the confetti settled, the flashbulbs dimmed and the champagne corks fell to earth, Walter found himself facing the dilemma that always follows a career-best album. Where next? His answer was a curveball. If Modern Daze had been an album that prized original songwriting over all else, then its follow-up was the conceptual antithesis.

"I've always loved the act of writing a new song," explains Walter. "It's something I've done for as long as I've been doing this, because a lot of times, I can't find cover songs that say what I'm feeling. So Luther's Blues was my first-ever covers album."

In fact, this latest album had been

almost three decades in the making, ever since Walter shared a high-altitude lunch in 1986 with the Chicago bandleader Luther Allison at the Alpine chalet of Montreux Jazz Festival founder Claude Nobs.

"I already had some of Luther's earlier albums," explains Walter. "But when I met him, he was hooking up with Ruf and starting to make the later albums that are really his classic stuff. He was hitting his peak, and he was the warmest, most amazing human being. Like me, his career got started in Europe, and we kinda bonded over that."

Opposite: The Life Of Riley, the documentary film about blues legend, B.B. King, gets the Trout seal of approval at the World Premiere in London on October 12, 2012
Above: After the film, Walter hosts a jam session featuring (among others) former Rolling Stone, Mick Taylor

A friendship and mutual respect snowballed, as evidenced by the touching sleeve-shot of Luther's Blues, in which the two men stand arm-in-arm, having just shared the Jazz Fest stage in 1986. "When Luther got up to play with us that year," recalls Walter, "it was a pretty astounding dose of energy. That show was incredible, but it turned out to be the only time I ever played with him. In the mid-'90s, he was just starting to achieve major recognition here in the States, and that was his dream. He was headlining all the major festivals, he was on the cover of all the magazines, he swept the W.C. Handy Awards. He'd really arrived, and was being toasted by the fans and critics. Then he got cancer. He was diagnosed, and he was gone three weeks later.

"It was just a really tragic thing. And ever since Luther died, back in 1997, I kinda feel like he's been forgotten by the press and blues radio. I'm not pointing the finger at anyone, but that kinda pissed me off. So I had thought about recording this covers album for years. It was just time to do it."

Luther's Blues wasn't about note-perfect recital, explains Walter, but spit, grit and spirit: "We did it at Entourage

with Eric again, and up until a couple of days before, I hadn't even picked the songs. I knew Luther's work inside-out, but to pick just twelve songs was difficult. The album was a sorta last-minute thing.

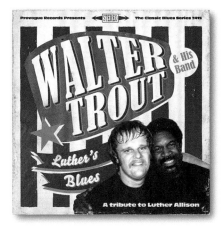

I came up with a list of tunes, took them in there with the band all set up, and just said, 'OK, here's how it goes'. My awesome band of Sammy, Rick and Michael did their stuff in three days. With this kind of music, that spontaneity is important."

Released in June 2013, Luther's Blues was another huge success, later picked out by the Classic Rock Blues Magazine as an album of the year and doubtless

informing the decision of the British Blues Awards to crown Walter Overseas Artist Of The Year. "My wife always compares making an album to having a child," notes Walter. "Y'know, you carry the child a certain amount of months, then out it comes, and even if it looks like a big toe, to you it's the most beautiful thing in the world. But it's nice to get some positive outside reaction. Of course, with a kid, nobody would say, 'What an ugly child…'"

For Walter, the real triumph of Luther's Blues wasn't the units shifted or the statuettes, but the spreading of the word. "Most people weren't even really aware of the songs I picked," he explains. "But I remember doing an interview after that album came out and the guy said to me, 'Well, I've never heard the original Cherry Red Wine, but as soon as we hang up, I'm gonna go check it out'. That made me feel great. I wanted people to go back and check out the master. That was the whole point of that album."

Above: On stage with Luther Allison at the Montreux Jazz Festival, 1986
Opposite top: Backstage with Luther Allison at the Montreux Jazz Festival, 1986
Opposite bottom: Walter and his prized photo of Luther

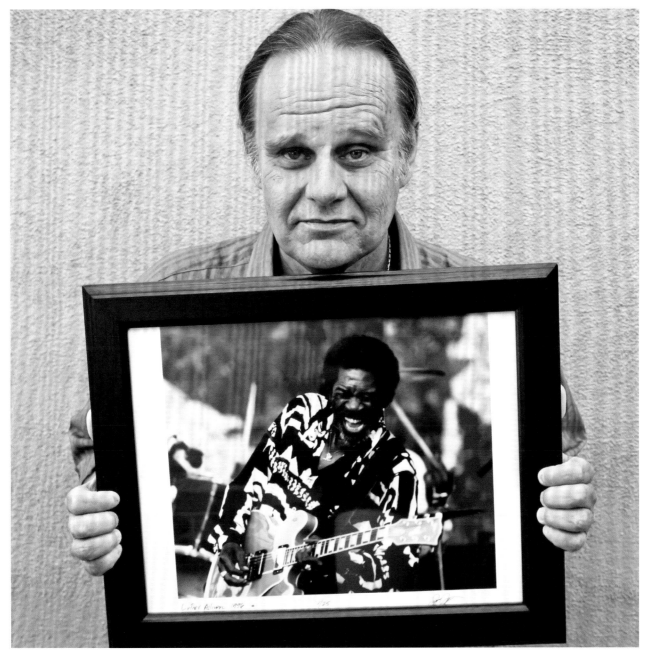

A stunning portrait of the artist at work by Theo Reijnders

GO THE DISTANCE

Bold plans were afoot. Record company wheels were in motion. 2014 was to be the year of the Trout, and Mascot's release schedule suggested there would never be a party like it, with Walter's quarter-century solo anniversary to be toasted by a starburst of commemorative offerings. Ten of his classic albums would be reissued on enhanced quality 180 gram vinyl. An expansive official biography – this one – and a documentary film would dig back into his astonishing life story, before a new studio album and world tour charged headlong into the next chapter.

Then one night in June 2013 changed the script. "I was on tour in Germany," remembers Walter. "I woke up one night, bloated and puffed-up with fluid. My legs looked like telephone poles. I had to finish the tour sitting on a chair, then I came home and found out I have a liver disease that had caused some cirrhosis of the liver.

"My liver was barely functioning, and that throws my whole digestive tract off. I was 230 pounds, now I'm down to around 130. I'm on medication that gives me an eighty per cent chance of stopping the liver disease and thus halting the spread of the cirrhosis. Now, if that doesn't work, then I fight on, try something else."

Having travelled eleven chapters alongside him, we already know Walter as a man who specialises in battles against cruel fate, yet his bravery in 2013 was something else. Scan the tour diary and it's extraordinary to note that the bandleader cancelled just three shows in the immediate aftermath of that night in Germany, crossed the States through the summer, then returned to Europe for triumphant dates in October and November. Night after night, venue after venue, Walter siphoned the crowd's adoration and sprayed it back as molten blues-rock magic. The sympathy vote didn't even come into it.

"There was a point when I was laying around feeling sorry for myself," he admits. "Saying that I didn't think I could do it, blah blah blah. And it was Marie who said, 'Y'know, the most healing thing you can do for your spirit right now is to go out, play for people and make that connection. So I went out there, very apprehensively. She was precisely right. By the end of that tour, I just felt rejuvenated and in a great frame of mind. I've not just been surprised by the support people have given me. I've been overwhelmed."

> It was Marie who said, 'Y'know, the most healing thing you can do for your spirit right now is to go out, play for people and make that connection. She was precisely right. By the end of that tour, I just felt rejuvenated and in a great frame of mind. I've not just been surprised by the support people have given me. I've been overwhelmed.

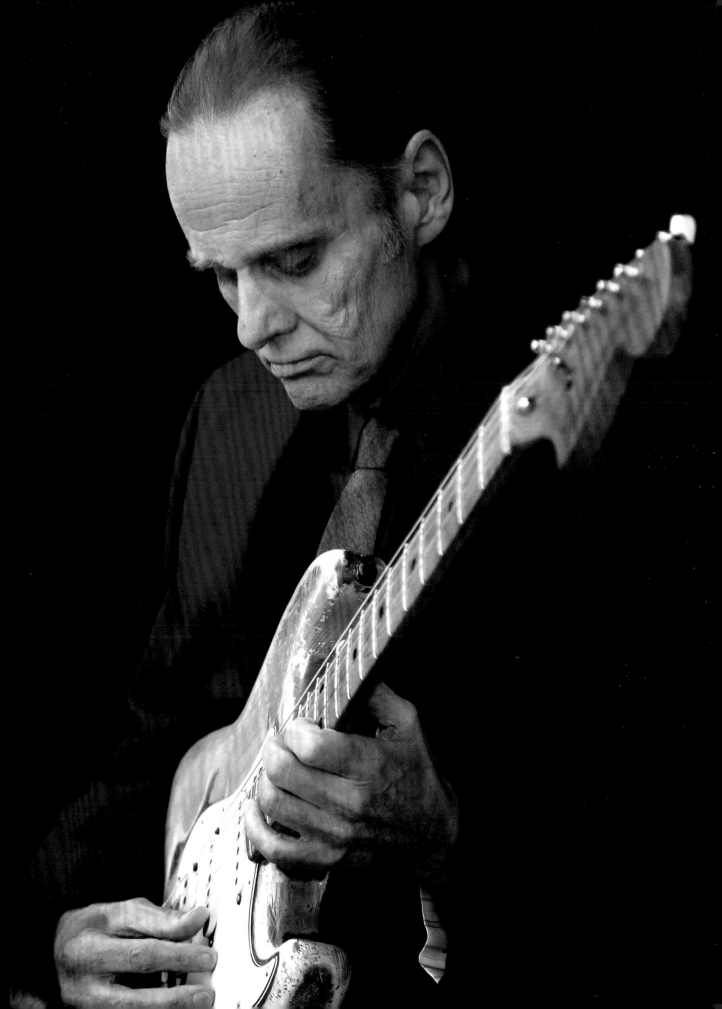

By happy coincidence, Walter's UK dates dovetailed with the annual awards ceremony of British hard-rock bible, Classic Rock, and on November 14th, he stepped onto the stage at London's Roundhouse to introduce John Mayall. Appropriately enough, the Bluesbreakers leader was there to collect a Classic Album award for the Beano record that had changed both their lives.

"That was amazing," says Walter. "I had a big speech prepared, but in the end I just thought, I'm gonna shorten it way down. So I said, 'When you devote your life to playing the blues, you do it not because you're looking for money, fame or ego, but because the music is in your blood and in your soul, because it moves you, and you love it more than

> **When you devote your life to playing the blues, you do it not because you're looking for money, fame or ego, but because the music is in your blood and in your soul, because it moves you, and you love it more than anything else on the fucking planet.**

anything else on the fucking planet'. Then I said, 'As this man does…' – and I brought up John Mayall.

"After you present the award," he adds, "they escort you through this maze of interviews and photographers, and while Mayall and I are waiting to get our photo taken, right next to me is Jimmy Page. He turns to me and says, 'Oh, Walter Trout, I've heard your work and I think it's wonderful'. I thought to myself real quick and instead of bowing down, I said, 'Hey, Jimmy Page. I've heard your work too… and I think it's fucking wonderful too'. He started laughing, this big grin on his face, like he hadn't heard that one before."

As 2013 played out, Walter juggled the activity of his anniversary year with the

demands of his condition. He continued to give extensive interviews for the book you're holding.

He participated in the aforementioned film documentary directed by Frank Duijnisveld. Above all, he manfully chipped away at the album sessions that had started in April, now channeling the events of the past six months as his guiding theme.

"I chose to call the album The Blues Came Callin'," explains Walter, "because it was pretty much written and recorded in the midst of this illness. I actually think the album has come out great. I think I've come through with one of the most rocking records of my whole career. There's hardly a slow song on there. It's blues-rock at its most raw and

elemental. Real balls-out, primal scream kinda stuff. There's a sense of me trying to get some feelings off my chest about what's happened to me, because it's pretty severe."

Beyond that overt album title, you only had to scan the track listing to sense a man squaring up to his circumstances. "Some of the songs are blatant and in-your-face. I have one called Wastin' Away. The lyric goes, 'I look in the mirror, I don't know who I see. I take another look, but it still don't look like me'. I'm skin and bone now.

"I wear these sweat pants that I tie up over the protuberance of the fluid, so if I'm out walking and they ride down past that shelf, they fall down immediately. Quite a few times, I've caught them

when they've been around my knees, at the shopping mall or something. It makes it quite exciting to be out in public trying to hold your pants up, y'know?

"Then there's the title track, which is pretty gut-wrenching. It's me trying to deal with the reality of my situation. It's metaphorical, but it tells the story of how I lay in bed and the blues creeps in through the window, grabs a hold of me and says into my ear, 'You'll never be the man you used to be'.

Opposite and Above: Walter and British jazz legend, Chris Barber present John Mayall with the Classic Album Award at the *Classic Rock* Roll of Honour at The Roundhouse on November 14, 2013 in London, England

This spread: Despite his health issues, Walter delivers another breathtaking performance to an ecstatic crowd at the Tivoli in Utrecht, 19 November, 2013

"Another important one is The Bottom Of The River. I wrote it as a metaphor about a man who goes out on a boat, falls in, and the current pulls him to the bottom. Above, he sees the light on the surface, but it's too hard to fight the current. Then he sees his life pass before his eyes: all the people he's loved and done wrong, all the places he's left and belonged. He realises he wants more, that he's not going to give up. At that moment, he finds all his strength and fights to the surface. As he crawls out, he sees beauty in the world he never saw before, and realises it's changed him profoundly. I'm really proud of that song. But it's almost hard for me to listen to."

The metaphor, of course, is the thinnest of veils for Walter's own renewed appreciation: "I see beauty around me now that I never noticed before, or that I maybe took for granted. I know the world is a cruel and violent place, but underneath it all, I see man's humanity and the beauty of the ecosystem; the birds, the trees, the wind, the sun. I lay in bed at night; I can hear waves breaking in the distance, in the Pacific, and I think of all the creatures going through their lives, and I think what an incredibly complex, beautiful, magnificent creation this world is. I didn't see any of that before."

Music, too, had never sounded sweeter. Far from a contract-fulfilling grind, Walter found sessions for The Blues Came Callin' a morale-boosting catharsis. "Music, for me, has always been the equivalent to going to a shrink, laying on a couch and baring your soul. I did the new record with Eric again. He's become my musical partner and alter-ego, and if I live another twenty years and make eighteen more albums, I can't see me working with anybody else. We're a perfect team. He just intrinsically gets what I'm trying to do. We mainly did the

album at Entourage, then I did some overdubbing of vocals and guitars at Clear Lake in Hollywood, and a few days of just singing vocals at The Lion's Den, which is Eric's studio."

Alongside the bedrock Trout band, several old faces blew through the sessions. "Deacon plays organ on a Canned Heat-style boogie called Willie that I wrote about the many people in my life who had ripped me off. We also did two tracks with John Mayall that were great fun. He walked in and I said, 'John, I want you to do two things today that

you don't do on record anymore. Number one, I want you to play the Hammond B3, because you always play your little synthesiser, but on the Beano album you're playing B3 and it sounds great'. With that slow-blues title track, we just counted to four and played it live, right there in the studio. Later, I went back and redid the vocal, but the instrumental track is completely cut live: one take.

"Then I said to John, 'Number two, I've heard you sitting around in your living room playing boogie-woogie piano, and you're really good at it, but you never do it on record'. At which point, John walked over to the piano, sat down, and thank God, Eric was there to push record. John started off and one by one, me, the bass player and drummer kinda shuffled into the room and joined in. A totally

spontaneous one-take no-rehearsal jam! I've called it Mayall's Piano Boogie."

Tracking didn't always come so easy. "It got a little funky at times. Every other album I've done, I've gone up to LA every day for two weeks: start, finish, boom, it's done. The Blues Came Callin' took months. I started having these severe health problems where I had to be in the hospital for days, and go back and forth. In January 2014, I was taken to the ER, on the verge of having a seizure and maybe dying. So it was day-by-day. I'd have rough days where I couldn't breathe. I'd have days where I'd shake so bad I couldn't get the food to my mouth, because it's falling off the fork. Marie would literally have to spoon feed me. I'd drive up to the studio and only be good for two hours, then I'd have to come home because I had no energy left. I spent longer driving than I did recording."

At times, you hear the context in Walter's performances. "I sang that album with the illness and it has changed my voice," he explains. "So I sound different on this record, but the emotion, soul and desire to express myself are all there. As for the playing, I did some of the original sessions in April 2013, before all this happened, and the guitar on that is blazing. The stuff I've overdubbed since then, I'm really happy with, but I had to work on it. Sometimes I'd go up there and say to Eric, 'I just can't play today'. Other days, I'd go, 'OK, let's milk it while I got it'. Then I'd play until I couldn't play anymore. Marie said to me that it added some urgency and emotional intensity."

Above: Once upon a time, it was reel after reel of tape but today it's hours and hours of takes on CD that Walter's refined ears go to work on to get the The Blues Came Callin' album sounding just right

The Blues Came Callin' runs the emotional gamut, its songs tearing between eloquent defiance, anger, sorrow and uncertainty. But regret? That's a more slippery commodity, as Walter explains: "Knowing what I know now, I would not have followed the same path. But that's easy to say now. I mean, my liver is fried, through heroin and alcohol, and of course, it would be nice to have a wonderful, pristine, Disneyland kind of liver. But I don't want to say, 'I regret this', or 'I regret that'. Because I feel like I'm able to put some feeling, emotion and experience – maybe even a tiny bit of knowledge and wisdom – into my music, that if I'd lived a Disneyland life wouldn't be there.

"There has to be a story there to tell," he considers. "There are some young guys out there where it's all technique. I'd rather hear some beat-up old black guy who's had years of homelessness and is playing on a $25 guitar – but when he plays that one note, it makes you weep. I listen to music to hear the artist's story and message. I want the nitty-gritty, right from his heart and soul. That's why I can't stand the whole persona thing. I don't want to know who Ziggy Stardust is. I want to know who the fuck David Bowie is."

Heart and soul. Run a survey on the door and you'd most likely find those twin factors cited by the punters who stream in every time the Trout band rolls into town. On a purely visceral level, of course, the music moves their feet, but it's more than that: by telling his own story, the man onstage is articulating every hope and fear in the house. If this is therapy, then it flows both ways. "We've always had this little saying in my band," notes Walter, "that we are the people's band. We all laugh about it, but we take it very seriously, too. I can't stand that whole thing of, 'I'm up here playing and you people are lucky you're even on the same planet'. I can't stand that bullshit.

"I want my fans to know that I'm one of them. We happen to play instruments, but other than that, we're just the same. We're no better than anybody else. We're struggling, just like they're struggling. Everybody in that crowd is fighting a battle, just to get through this life and this world. So with The Blues Came Callin', I wanted to share my feelings, because I know there are other people out

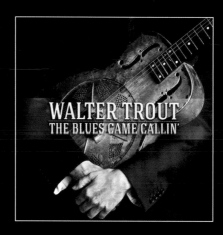

It's a tough fight, a big fight, a long fight. But I'm ready for it. I'll take it on. Because what I have is worth fighting for, and I have learned that anything that is truly worthwhile in life is worth fighting for. When I look at my family, my career, my life, how I came through it all, what I've achieved and what I have in my life – I feel like I'm the luckiest man alive.

there in the crowd who are going through the same thing. It may not be able to help them, but it can certainly say to them, 'I understand'. We're all going through the same shit together. We don't have any answers for you, but we're asking the same questions that you're asking."

As these closing words are written, the most pressing questions from Walter's global fan base concern his future and medical prognosis. This book cannot answer them, of course, and neither can

the bandleader himself. In any case, if Walter has learnt anything from his travels, it's that somebody up there is calling the shots. "I remember going to John Mayall a few times back in the Bluesbreakers," he says, "sitting there all fucked-up, and telling him, 'John, I've had a revelation. I've heard the voice of whatever greater power you want to call it and it said to me that if I showed the strength of character to quit drugs and booze, then God would give me the desire of my heart'.

"Back then, I thought that was gonna be megastardom. I thought that would mean I would be up there with Eric Clapton and the Stones. But what I didn't realise was that the true desire of my heart, really, was to have the one thing I'd never had in my life, which was a loving family. Because although I did have loving parents, it was the most dysfunctional family you can imagine. That voice I heard told me the truth, because I did give up the dope and the booze – and I was given love and children."

This book began with one vision of paradise, on the endless beach of an idyllic island resort. It ends with another, in the home of a family bound together by love. And now, having rescued him from reality, it is that same family who give Walter Trout the impetus and courage to walk on. "The last year has changed me," he concludes. "It's brought me much closer to my wife and my children. It's shown me just how dear they are to me, and how much I would love to go on. So I'm fighting like a son of a bitch. I'm not giving in. It's on me to fight this, to beat it, and hopefully have another twenty years of watching my kids grow and making music.

"You play with the hand you're dealt, and you do your best to win the game. It's a tough fight, a big fight, a long fight. But I'm ready for it. I'll take it on. Because what I have is worth fighting for, and I have learned that anything that is truly worthwhile in life is worth fighting for. When I look at my family, my career, my life, how I came through it all, what I've achieved and what I have in my life – I feel like I'm the luckiest man alive."

THE BOTTOM OF THE RIVER

I went out on the river
Way outside of town
I fell into the water
And the current pulled me down
It held me on the bottom
I could not hear a sound
I was lost in muddy water
And I thought that I would drown

Somewhere up above me
I could see the light
I knew I had to reach it
It was just too hard a fight
The current flowed around me
I felt the end was near
My mind filled up with memories
And my heart filled up with fear
I couldn't see before me
It was cloudy – it was cold
At the bottom of the river
Is where I met my soul

Then I saw my life before me
And I knew I wanted more
And I understood so many things
I didn't understand before
I saw all the people I had loved
And all I had done wrong
And the places I had left behind
And the places I belonged
Then I heard a voice inside me
It sounded like a cry
I heard it scream so loudly
This ain't your time to die

That's when I decided
To make it to the light
I found the strength inside me
And I fought with all my might
I made it to the surface
I was gasping for my breath
And I cried in realization
That I had cheated death
I noticed so much beauty
As I crawled up on the shore
That day I changed forever
From who I was before

Writing this book has been a bitter-sweet journey for me, lots of laughs and lots of tears! I want to give a special thank you to Henry Yates for doing such a great job of diligently and carefully linking all the pieces and tidbits of my life into a coherent narrative.

All in all, it's been surreal to come face to face with events from my past-some of which I had tried hard to forget. As I read back over the pages and experience my life in review, there are many things I wish I had done differently.

But regrets get us nowhere! All we can do is to learn from the past and live our lives differently in the future.

I do know that my youth seemed to be a dead-end! And I felt completely out of touch – a misfit. My reality was one of loneliness, confusion, and fear. When I discovered music, I discovered my sanctuary.

I discovered my Cathedral! Music was and always will be my refuge. My release. My rescue from reality.

Walter Trout, April 2014

ACCESS ALL AREAS

From the very early days of Wilmont Mews right up to the present day, writing music, touring and playing live is what it's all about for Walter. But the good ship Trout can't sail without a world-class crew and these guys are the best in the business.

MARIE TROUT
MANAGER (1993-PRESENT)

She's his wife, lover, muse and soulmate – but it's her management genius that's kept Walter's career on top for two decades. Take a bow, Marie Trout…

On the fateful night she floated through the crowd in Denmark, Walter Trout saw in Anne Marie Bech Brændgaard a soulmate, not a prospective manager. And yet, within three years, this tack-sharp former advertising executive had dispensed with the villains bleeding the bluesman and resurrected his career.

"I did tour managing from 1991 to late-1992," explains Marie, "and then I took over management in 1993. Walter was hurt by his ex-managers' deceit and felt stranded. He didn't know who he could trust. I knew that my background of owning a small advertising sales company was perfect to help him. I told him we could make all the big decisions together and I'd handle the day-to-day planning and executing.

"The first tour we did after firing Walter's old management in 1993 brought in enough money for us to pay our expenses and start saving for a house," she continues. "We didn't have to pawn Walter's guitars to pay rent anymore.

Knowing our combined efforts made that possible was incredibly gratifying. I loved seeing the joy in Walter's face as he realized he was now not just making music, he was also making enough money to raise a family."

The wife/manager is typically represented in popular culture as a ball-breaking harpy. "It's a misnomer!" laughs Marie. "This is teamwork. Walter has a strong vision of what he wants to do creatively. I help him put that into action. I help his ideas materialize. I negotiate record deals and touring fees. I plan and coordinate the touring, and work with publicists, labels and booking agents. I do budgets, social media, accounting, keep track of expenses and band fees. I get up at 3am and make phone calls to Europe. I basically take on the nitty-gritty work behind the scenes so he can focus on being plugged into the universe and allow the music to just flow through him.

"My interests in music and therapy have been crucial to the job," she adds.

"I was raised in a very musical family: I trained for ten years in violin and piano, and took music education in high school. I have a keen interest in psychology and wanted to be a psychologist or therapist, which formed my choices in college. To do this job, you also need an ego that can survive in the back-seat. As an artist's manager, you're basically invisible. You may work day and night on an album project or tour, and nobody ever says, 'Wow, what a great job!'"

Yet amidst the hard work, stresses Marie, there are untouchable highs. "The best part of this role is helping Walter to be Walter. To make sure he has a platform from which he can do what he does best. Walter has a way of helping people feel seen. To feel connected to themselves – and to others. To help from the sidelines, to make this magic possible, is my greatest professional joy."

Opposite: Tour manager Marie shares a beer with a friend in 1991 at an outdoor festival in Denmark

THE BAND AND CREW

ANDREW ELT
EUROPE TOUR MANAGER (2000-PRESENT)

The show must go on – and ensuring it does falls to Andrew Elt. Having led major-label glam-metallers Sleeze Beez in the '80s and '90s, he met Walter while fronting a Beatles tribute in 2000, and joined the band as tour manager three weeks later. "I thought, what the hell, I'll give it a go," he remembers. "First show in Amsterdam, I had to go on after the third encore to tell the audience Walter wasn't coming back. The crowd was getting rowdy and no one dared go out there. Walter said, 'Don't worry, Andrew will do it…!'"

Fourteen years later, Andrew is the fixer, wheel-greaser and backline guru, who keeps the bus rolling and the live sound rocking (not to mention his nightly vocal cameo on songs like Mercy and Goin' Down). "The testing part is that every show is different technically," he explains. "We don't tour with our own lights and sound, so it's always a challenge to see what the venues have to work with. But as far as the horror stories go, this band is a walk in the park. There's no drink and drugs, so they're always on time!"

There are other challenges: "Going to India with Walter was an experience. They lost the band's luggage on arrival, including amps and keyboards. Our first trip to Lithuania, we had a sixteen-hour delay.

"Also, Walter is a chronic insomniac, and any noise, creak or flutter will keep him up. One night, he couldn't sleep and decided the air-con was making a funny noise, so he borrowed my screwdriver and took it apart completely. Only to find out the noise was coming from the air-con next door…"

MICHAEL LEASURE
DRUMS (2008-PRESENT)

With a gold-plated résumé that includes Albert Collins, Buddy Miles and Edgar Winter, California-born sticksman Michael Leasure was ready for the challenge of the Trout band. "I joined in March 2008," he recalls, "but I was a fan of Walter's music long before that. When I first heard him on the radio, I said to myself, 'That's the kinda band I need to play with: high-energy, balls-out blues-rock, with room to stretch and express myself musically'.

"A few years later, I was standing next to my old buddy Sammy Avila, who happened to be talking to Walter, so I grabbed the phone and said, 'Hey Walter, my name is Mike Leasure and I'm your next drummer!' Six months later, he needed a drummer and the rest, as they say, is history."

To watch Michael live is to witness a percussion master playing in the moment. "Drumming is so much more than keeping a beat," he explains. "It's feel, dynamics, emotion, having complete awareness of the song at all times. Why? Because Walter plays from his soul and never plays a song the same way twice. Also, he never uses a setlist, so we're always on our toes. It took a bit of time to learn his body language and other nuances onstage, but we play together without thinking now, and that's when it's the best."

Another key demand is knowing how to take a joke. "About a month after Walter hired me," recalls Michael, "he called me on April Fools' Day and fired me. Man, I was pissed! I thought everything was going great. Totally had me on the hook. He strung me along for about ten minutes, then busted out laughing. We laugh about it now. I'll get him back…"

RICK KNAPP
BASS (2005-PRESENT)

Rewind to 2005, and filling the vacated shoes of the fallen Jimmy Trapp was a challenge to make most bassists quake. Not so Rick Knapp, who swept up the gauntlet with the confidence you'd expect of a lifer who had scattered fairy-dust over the work of artists like Stephen Stills, Bo Diddley and Sam Lay.

"I first saw Walter in a club in 2003," remembers the Indiana-born musician, who is also a solo artist and hugely talented guitarist in his own right. "I was blown away with his aggressive musical onslaught. In the break, I told him I'd played much of my career with legendary Chicago blues artists, then handed him the phone number of my old boss and mentor, the great drummer Sam Lay from the Paul Butterfield Band. After a conversation with Sam, Walter invited me to sit in, and I officially joined the band in 2005."

Rick brought masterful low-end, but just as vital was the personal dynamic. "As I came to know Walter," he says, "it became very apparent we shared much common ground in perspectives, attitudes and music. During the insanity of this extreme touring grind, the blues renegade hippie wild-man became my dear friend. I love him and I love the music. As I reflect upon the last decade, I realise the depth of connection shared within this experience, from finding and marrying my first love Beverly after 43 years, to recording and performing alongside some of the greatest blues icons, to standing on Red Square in Moscow at midnight.

"I grew up in the rural farmland of Indiana, and Walter in a big East Coast city. Funny, it ain't really that far apart…"

SAMMY AVILA
KEYBOARDS (2001-PRESENT)

Raised in the San Gabriel Valley and rocking the Los Angeles club circuit, Sammy Avila knew the West Coast scene and had admired Walter Trout's work from afar. "I heard his music on the radio, then went to buy a couple of his CDs," remembers the keys wizard. "Wow. What a great guitar player. Knowing his history and all he's done up till now has been fabulous."

Familiarity with the Trout back catalogue proved useful too, when Sammy returned home one night in 2001 to discover the admiration was mutual. "I listened to my phone messages that evening and there was one from Walter asking for me. He'd got my number from a guitar player friend of mine, Joey Delgado. I called Walter and he invited me to sit in with the band. I went down to Perqs in Huntington Beach and played two songs with him and the band. It was so fun. Next day, he called and asked me to join the band – and it's been an adventure ever since."

Thirteen years later, Sammy's searing virtuosity is a vital element in the studio and on the stage. "I love to play, and to be able to burn it up every gig has been a blast," he explains. "All the guys playing hard makes me play hard. One of my greatest high-points in the band was when we recorded the Relentless DVD/CD in Amsterdam, and sharing the stage with B.B. King at the Pacific Amphitheater back in 2011 was a great time. Sharing life and music with Walter has been a joy. We get along really good. He's just a nice guy – and so funny…"

PHIL CASEBERRY
US TOUR MANAGER (1991-PRESENT)

"I first met Walter in 1991," remembers Phil Caseberry. "I was working for a PA company who were supplying sound for some of Walter's UK shows. The band at that time was Walter, Jimmy, Mongo and Frank Cotinola. There was a lot of joking around, but when those guys hit the stage it was all business. Boy, does he play a mean guitar."

Walter aside, only Phil remains from that early solo lineup, though his role has evolved since 1991. "I did monitors for a lot of the UK shows for four years," he explains, "and in 1995 I was asked to tour with the band in Europe doing front-of-house. So since 1995, I've done FOH, backline and driving, and in the last few years, in the USA, I've taken over tour managing duties from Andrew. On the whole, the FOH and backline parts are pretty easy-going; it just gets a bit stressful when long drives are involved. The tour managing is a whole different ballgame – that can be very hectic."

But he wouldn't change it: "I've seen 23 of the 25 years of Walter's solo career close-up, and it's been a hell of a ride. There have been some great times travelling with Walter and the band over the years. Festivals with Page & Plant and Status Quo.

"Going to Moscow. Niagara Falls in the winter and the chaos of Mumbai. My favourite, though, was riding my bike from the UK up to Norway and Denmark for a long weekend at the Notodden and Skanderborg festivals. After hearing my bike roar off down the fjords, Walter exclaimed, 'Jesus, Philip, don't you ever tell me my guitar is too loud again!'"